W9-DBU-125

The

Low-Upkeep Book

of

Lawns and Landscape

By Elvin McDonald and Lawrence Power:
  Garden Ideas A to Z

By Elvin McDonald:
  The Complete Book of Gardening under Lights
  The Flowering Greenhouse Day by Day
  Handbook for Greenhouse Gardeners
  Miniature Plants for Home and Greenhouse
  The World Book of House Plants

THE

LOW-UPKEEP BOOK

OF

LAWNS AND LANDSCAPE

by

Elvin McDonald

and

Lawrence Power

A Helen Van Pelt Wilson Book

HAWTHORN BOOKS, INC.

Publishers

New York

Designed by Harold Franklin

1 2 3 4 5 6 7 8 9 10

ACKNOWLEDGMENTS

Special thanks to landscape architects Robert Zion, Thomas Church, William L. Koenig, and Leon Goldberg for the plans and advice they contributed; Dr. James Watson, Chief Agronomist at Toro Manufacturing Company, for technical assistance on the lawn chapters; architect Dale Booher and designer Robert Bray, for changing blueprints into line drawings for reproduction; David Hunter for artwork; Jacqueline Hunter for assistance with the tools chapter; Alice Skelsey for providing a wealth of material from the United States Department of Agriculture; Professor Wayne H. Wilson, head of the School of Landscape Architecture, Pennsylvania State University, and his able staff, for spending the better part of a Saturday showing us photographs of contemporary residential landscaping.

Deep appreciation to our enduring and encouraging editor, Helen Van Pelt Wilson, with whom we carried on spirited debates; and to copy editor Dan Walden, who so ably did the final work on our manuscript.

E. M.
L. P.

New York City

CONTENTS

CHAPTER I

THE LOW-UPKEEP
CONCEPT

Instant foods, easy-care furnishings, miracle fabrics, less-work appliances—convenience is the key to our current life-style. Since trends in applied arts such as landscaping are invariably the result of social and economic factors, it is only natural that landscape architects would develop low-upkeep techniques that relate closely to the way we live.

For many "weekends-are-to-relax" homeowners, gardening is not a pastime. It is work—work that we must do ourselves, since the scarcity and high cost of labor have ruled out outside help.

Landscaping is also work that cannot be ignored. The glass walls of modern architecture have increased its importance. They make the outdoors an integral part of our interior living. When the barbecue craze swept the country after World War II, it introduced the outdoors as an extension of inside space. Dining al fresco has since become an American institution.

Industry has also had a major influence in molding current landscaping techniques. Because architects specified plantings to humanize contemporary offices, businessmen took a dollar-wise look at landscaping. Their evaluation showed that maintenance costs exceed the initial cash outlay for plant materials and installation in less than five years. As a result, industry demanded and got good landscaping with built-in low maintenance. The solutions developed for commercial landscaping are now being applied to our residential needs and the result is a new concept in home landscaping—the low-upkeep concept.

In this book our concern with low maintenance does not, however, dismiss the pleasures of making things grow. We merely attempt to minimize the toil. Actually, the low-upkeep concept should increase the general interest in gardening. With the greater part of the garden organized for easy care, there's more time for specialized pursuits—cutting flowers, espaliering fruit trees, or planning a summer garden party. Although the trend to low-maintenance designing is established with professionals, don't expect a look at your neighbor's property to be inspiring. If America were evaluated on the present state of its home landscaping, there is little doubt that it would be declared a disaster area.

The current suburban landscaping practice is to center the house on a lot. This leaves no one area that is really large enough for outdoor living. The house is then fringed with a foundation planting and the rest of the property planted in grass. This landscaping looks sparse in the beginning, soon becomes overgrown, and views from the house are cut off. Space is wasted on a high-maintenance lawn that is seldom used, except for your walking across it untold thousands of times mowing, feeding, and weeding.

Only one step beyond this is today's mass-produced so-called professional landscaping job, which consists of a free-form island of trees midway in the front yard, mulched with pebbles or gravel. Granted, this sometimes works beautifully. But unless the islands are handled with real style or integrated into the rest of the landscape, they should be left in the ocean where islands belong rather than the middle of your suburban lawn.

The quality of neighborhood landscaping seems to have a snow-balling effect. Once a precedent is set, whether good or bad, it is followed by one homeowner after another. We imitate what we see. Unfortunately, what we see is more than likely bad.

Well-designed properties in this country are apparently restricted to those planned and planted by competent landscape architects or knowledgeable owners. Most owners who feel the need of professional help seek the advice of the local nurseryman rather than pay for an architect's services. Nurserymen are experts in propagating and growing plants but they do not necessarily have the sense of design or level of taste to set them up as arbiters of style. Also, the view of the nurseryman, whose business is selling plants, is not exactly unbiased. Whether you design your own property or hire a landscape architect, you'll get the best results if you yourself have a basic knowledge of design and low-upkeep methods.

A broad planting of English ivy and a path of crushed stone have been used to reduce grass area and separate the formal entrance from the play yard. Moraine locusts give a sense of airiness and play of shadows. Landscaping by Goldberg and Rodler. *Mal Gurian Assoc. photo.*

BEGIN PLANNING EARLY

The first step in landscaping is always planning. For best results, your planning should begin before the contractor sites the house, does the major grading, places walkways, drives, and parking area. A house cannot be built without a professional plan, but most contractors proceed without professional advice when it comes to the outside. Of course, there are a few builders who employ landscape architects. But the typical contractor is concerned only with getting the site cleared as quickly as possible,

Large pots of annuals, with an autumn change to chrysanthemums, add color to family eating and entertaining on this suburban terrace. The plantings are a snap to change with the season. If you want to coordinate colors, match the flowers to your table mats or china. Robert Zion, L. A. *Alexandre Georges photo.*

4

the house up, the deed in your name, a check in his hand, and his men and equipment moved on. His motivation is purely financial and a tree that took twenty to thirty years in the growing can bite the dust in three minutes in the wake of his bulldozer.

We will then approach designing for low upkeep from the ideal beginning: You are about to contract for a house to be built—you have paid or signed nothing. You are in your best bargaining position. Be careful not to sign over to the builder the right to remove "trees as necessary" or "site the house properly." If you fall into this trap, the game's probably lost.

In certain parts of the country, contractors are much more willing to make concessions than others. Regardless of where you live, don't be bullied by your builder. You are paying him. He may be unaccustomed to interference from prospective owners and may not like taking your advice, but let him know at the outset that *you* know what you want and intend to get it. Your own knowledge is your best defense.

Begin your planning with a family conference, and include all members. List the ways you might use the areas around your house. Think of more than making a good impression on arriving guests. Think about using the whole place for living and entertaining. The same kind of approach should be given to outdoor living space as the designer or architect gives to the interior.

Decide where the house should be placed, and where you want walkways and driveways. Are there any trees or plantings you want to save? Remember, the builder does have to have access for clearing the actual area to be covered by the house, but he needs only one driveway to come in and out, not two.

Make a basic plan, in scale, and present it to your builder. Don't take no for an answer. He may want an extra fee, but whatever it is, this will be cheaper than having trees destroyed, or having a house poorly sited, or other external construction done the wrong way. Whatever is done wrong in the beginning may seem like something you can "easily change later," but don't kid yourself. Landscape changes are expensive and time consuming. Most are never made.

A row of annuals (following bulbs), a dogwood tree, and a raised planting of evergreen shrubs give year-round color at the entrance to this Colonial house. William L. Koenig, L. A.

WORKING WITH EXISTING LANDSCAPING

For many of you, this advice comes too late. You may have purchased an older house with existing landscaping; your builder may already have cleared away everything, constructed the house, and put in cursory landscaping—grass seed sown or sod put down, a token foundation planting, and two shade trees if you were lucky.

If you have landscaping, recent or from a previous owner, be sure you know what you want and need before ripping things out, doing more planting, or attempting outdoor construction. The landscape you inherit is likely to be a high-maintenance trap. If so, first decide what plants you want to keep, then proceed, but slowly, making the changes that seem necessary. If possible, save any particularly beautiful plantings but be most concerned

A stained natural-wood fence screens the parking
area from this contemporary entrance-way. The
squares of plain and pebble concrete provide a low-
maintenance paving which adds interest to both
walk and driveway. *Western Wood Products Association photo.*

with the overall long-range appearance and the use of your property. Once you've put your plan on paper, put it into action. Transplanted city people often attach a sentimental value to every tree and bush they have. If your plantings are not useful or attractive or require heavy maintenance, they really must be rearranged or disposed of. Whether it is the driveway or a rosebush that isn't in the right place, move it or get rid of it.

MAINTENANCE TRAPS TO LOOK FOR

- Scattered plantings of shrubs or perennials, around the house, or here and there on the lawn.

- Attractive plantings wasted in places not readily visible from outdoor living areas or from windows inside.

- Large areas of lawn where grass isn't really needed for practical or esthetic reasons.

- Grass on any steep area difficult to mow.

- Small, broken-up lawn areas with sharp angles, which require extra backup work with the mower.

- Large, rampant shrubs near the house that require frequent prunings.

- Plants under a wide overhang where constant watering is needed since rain doesn't reach there.

- Trees of a kind subject to attacks by insects or diseases, or "dirty" trees that constantly drop leaves, bark, seeds, or fruit.

- Plants that are struggling or require extra attention to survive because they are tender for your region or just naturally miffy.

ESSENTIALS FOR THE LOW-UPKEEP LANDSCAPE

LAWNS.   Restrict grass to areas of play, for the formal entrance, or as a foreground for a flower border. Use edging strips to keep grass in a neat line out of flowerbeds and to avoid hand trimming. Plant ground-covers in heavy shade or excessively wet soil. Remove grass from around the base of trees; replace with gravel or stones. Get rid of small, chopped-up areas of grass and sharp angles difficult to mow. Use ground-cover on steep slopes. Install an automatic underground sprinkling system (not nearly so expensive as you imagine and such a comfort!).

FLOWERS. Depend on flowering shrubs, spring bulbs, and hardy perennials. Mass together. But not too many. Enough for impact outdoors. Mulch to avoid hand weeding. Use containers of annual-flowering plants for movable color—where you want it

Sun and fun are naturals on this redwood deck. Lawn care has been reduced and living space increased by cantilevering the deck on a sloping site. *Ezra Stoller, photo for California Redwood Association.*

There is little upkeep for the neat brick surface around this woodland swimming pool. The area has been cleared of trees to let in sun and to keep leaves out of the water. Planting beds are mulched with stones and wood chips. Landscaping by Goldberg and Rodler. *Mal Gurian Assoc. photo.*

at the moment. Don't fuss with a big flower garden otherwise. For cutting, grow in rows in a sunny, out-of-the-way corner where everything doesn't have to be kept in perfect order.

ENTRIES AND SIDE YARDS. Design with clean lines for a well-groomed look with little care. Select broadleaf and needle evergreens. In a side yard, or where there is a wide overhanging eave, mulch with pebbles, gravel, or woodchips. Result? Neat appearance, no upkeep.

DRIVEWAY AND PARKING AREA. Asphalt or concrete requires less maintenance than gravel. Gravel works away and has to be replaced. Bricks may also be used for an attractive surface. Place the parking area so it isn't on view from the house or from the outdoor living room. Outline the area with a bumper strip so that cars will not be driven onto grass. Light the drive and parking areas at night. If the driveway is long or difficult to navigate at night, install reflectors to assist.

PATIO, TERRACE, SUNDECK. Extend your house out into the landscape as far as possible by the use of permanent-surfaced outdoor living areas. Use wood, brick, stone, pebble-surfaced concrete, or tile to make the house seem larger and cut down on outside maintenance. Consider sun, shade, and the prevailing winds. Plan to eat in different spots. A terrace for breakfast or brunch should catch the morning sun. A terrace for noontime or early evening meals needs protection from southern and western sun. Terraces used in early spring and late fall need protection from chilling winds. Consider one large terrace for evening entertaining of a few friends, or a crowd—probably more people than you would ever have inside. Buy weatherproof furniture that doesn't have to be painted and won't rot. Avoid anything with cushions you have to take in at night or when it rains. If inexpensive aluminum and plastic furniture best fits your budget, select all in one color that blends into the landscape.

SWIMMING POOLS. Place a pool away from any trees that constantly drop leaves or seed pods, try to fit it naturally into the landscape, preferably so that your winter view from the house won't be directly into a frozen or canvas-covered pool. Design wide areas of permanent surfacing around the pool for sunning

The only thing square about this up-to-date sandbox and wading-pool combination is the shape. When the kids are bigger, the play boxes can be transformed into planting beds. *American Plywood Association photo.*

and eating. Pools require maintenance but this space might otherwise be in grass, which is no picnic either.

CHILDREN'S PLAY AREA. Should be on view from where you work in the house so that young children may be supervised from inside. Provide an open lawn space for rugged games but no grass under the swing set or around the sand pile. Instead, set down shredded bark or shingle-toe to save work. Plant shrubs without thorns, or screen with a solid fence such as redwood or stockade.

OUTDOOR COOKING.   Locate conveniently near the kitchen. Buy a small portable unit. Most places don't have space for a built-in barbecue pit with a chimney. More desirable today, a neat hibachi. All too often the outdoor cooking equipment becomes a focal point in the landscape. Be sure it isn't ugly. A small unit is easily cleaned and can be moved from one area to another to enable you to eat in different places depending on the occasion and the time of year. Avoid placing the unit over lawn grass because spilled lighter fluid discolors grass.

Eating and entertaining al fresco is a suburban ritual. An inexpensive portable cooking unit saves space and makes life easier for the chef. *American Plywood Association photo.*

TOOL STORAGE, GARDEN WORK CENTER, UTILITY.   Proper tools help keep garden work at a minimum. What you need is the right tool in good shape, stored where it belongs. Try to incorporate tool storage and a work center into a unit that also performs some landscape function—maybe to screen an unsightly view, garbage pails, a drying yard, or compost heap. Locate conveniently for moving the lawn mower, snow plow, and wheelbarrow. Design with permanent surfacing. Screen from public view and outdoor living area. This utility area can also incorporate a drying yard, a dog pen, and a place to store fireplace wood. Garbage cans recessed in the ground if possible. Plan a faucet in the area and night lighting.

A place for everything and everything in its place— that's the easy way to save time looking for garden tools. Fit the storage area into the landscape or screen it from view with trees or a fence. *American Plywood Association photo.*

CHAPTER II

MAKING

OR HIRING A PLAN

Before turning a spade of soil, put your landscape plan on paper. Once you have an accurate plot plan in black and white, you will be able to see the measured relationships of everything on your property. To do this you will need pencils, eraser, paper, and a ruler. It helps to have 24- x 36-inch graph paper, a pad of tracing paper the same size, a T-square, triangle, and compass. You will find these items at a stationery or art-supplies store. For measuring the property you will need a 100-foot tapemeasure, which will come in handy in countless ways as your real landscaping begins.

HOW TO MAKE A LANDSCAPE PLAN

If you can locate a survey or deed map, you will save hours of measuring, especially on a large property. This should be on file at your city hall, county courthouse, bank, mortgage, or title company. For a hillside site, you will need a contour map on which an engineer will have indicated contours in measurements of 1, 2, 5, or 10 feet.

It will also help if you can obtain the architect's or builder's drawings or house plans. These should include a site plan, floor plans, and elevations. By studying these you can determine the placement of doors, windows, roof lines, utilities, hose connections and outdoor electrical receptacles. In using such plans, check to be sure that siting was not changed in actual construction, or that windows, doors, or other structural details were not altered. Slight alterations may not be noticeable, yet they can make a tremendous difference in actual garden construction.

PUTTING YOUR PLAN ON PAPER. Depending on the size of your property, and the sheet of graph paper, decide on what scale to use. This might be ¼ inch to equal 1 foot, or 1 inch to equal 10 or 20 feet on a larger property. Various graph papers are divided

15

differently; you may be able to simply let one box equal 1 square foot.

Indicate on the map the locations of any existing buildings, driveways, walls, fences, walks, paths, major trees and shrubs, power lines, poles, easements, and right-of-ways. It is not necessary to draw in every tree and shrub, but rather you may indicate them as masses where they are grouped. It is useful to show the trunk placement of a large tree as well as the approximate branch spread. Indicate the direction North, so that patterns of sun and shade can be determined.

When this plan is complete, slip it under a sheet of tracing paper. Now you can sketch out ideas by the hour without messing up the master plan. When a completed new plan takes shape on a tissue overlay, transfer it to a new sheet of graph paper. When you consider it finished, have several photostatic copies made. You will need one for working with in the garden, one for inside, and one to take to the nursery when you buy. It won't hurt to have some extras.

By the time you reach the point of putting that first sheet of tissue over your master plan, you will have an accumulation of landscaping ideas in your head and also roughed out on notepaper. Doodling in miniature is an excellent way to try out a lot of ideas without feeling self-conscious as you may on a large sheet of tracing paper. Do final sketching to scale of any miniature that is appealing.

THE BASIC DESIGN.   As you plan, keep foremost in mind the low-upkeep concept. Within this framework, you want outdoor spaces that are livable and attractive. Strive for strong, clear design that will be pleasant to look at and live in. Professional landscape designers often define spaces by the use of wide mowing strips, raised planting beds, and low walls. These built-in features maintain the basic design even after years of plant growth. Think in terms of plant masses rather than specimens. Later, when the overall design is complete, you can decide where to put each plant of your choice.

USING CURVES.   Most landscape designs combine curves with right angles. Serpentine curves, crescents, and circles pleasantly lead the eye, and in a long narrow lot they can do all kinds of tricks to create illusions of space. Grass areas defined in curves make mowing easier.

THE MODULAR CONCEPT.   It is also possible to design partially or entirely within a modular concept, using only rectangles or squares. By this approach, you will take one basic unit, say 4 x 4 feet, and repeat it over and over. The patio could measure four 4-foot modules one way, seven the other, for a 16- x 28-foot total. One or more of the modules might be used as a planting pocket, the others paved. Walks and planting beds will be 4 feet wide, or in multiples of the basic 4 x 4 unit. If the modular approach appeals to you, try it. There may well be no quicker or easier way for you to achieve an attractive landscape design.

ELEVATION SKETCHES AND BUILDING A MODEL

For areas involving shrubs and trees or the construction of walls, fences, or buildings, it will be helpful to make elevation sketches. These show a two-dimensional view. For example, by working with the builder's elevation plans of your house, or large photos of it, you can make tissue overlays to try out various plant groupings in relation to a particular door or set of windows.

After you finish your complete design on paper, it may still be difficult for you to imagine how it will look in reality. Next best is to build a scale model. This is time-consuming but enjoyable work, especially in winter, and a far better way to discover faults in the plan than after it has been executed on the site in concrete, cash, and sweat. For the model you can use cardboard, clay, blocks of wood, bits of ceramic tile, evergreen clippings, and twigs.

WORKING WITH A LANDSCAPE ARCHITECT

If your property has special problems or you don't want to tackle the designing yourself, you may want to hire a landscape architect. If you already know a landscape designer who will be sympathetic to your wishes for livability and all-year good looks with a minimum amount of upkeep, you are fortunate. If not, check the Yellow Pages of your telephone directory for names of landscape architects. If none is listed, write for information to the American Society of Landscape Architects, 2000 K Street, N.W., Washington, D.C. 20006.

A landscape architect can be hired three ways: just to give advice, to draw a complete plan, or to handle the total job. The cost for design advice from a pro will pay for itself many times over, not only in pleasure derived from a plan that is initially well conceived, but also in lower maintenance costs.

If you approach a landscape architect whose work and reputation you do not know, ask to see "before" and "after" pictures of completed jobs. It doesn't take long to judge the quality and style and to decide if his designs are likely to be right for you.

ARCHITECTS' FEES. You pay the landscape architect a fee for his services, the same as you would a doctor or lawyer. He does not accept commissions or discounts from contractors, nurserymen, or dealers in materials, although his fee may be based on a percentage of the total *you* pay these suppliers.

The landscape architect's fee may be computed on an hourly basis for time devoted to your work, on a percentage of the total cost of planting and construction, or as a lump sum, agreed upon beforehand, or on a retainer.

THE LANDSCAPE ARCHITECT AS CONSULTANT. If you have the time and inclination to do most of the drawing and leg work for your own design, you may want a landscape architect only for an initial consultation to go over your land. His insight can be valuable. Thereafter you detail and execute the plans.

THE LANDSCAPE ARCHITECT AS PLANNER. You might have a landscape architect draw up complete plans for your place, but leave the execution of them to you. It is possible with any good plan to schedule the work in stages from season to season or year to year, depending on your budget of time and money.

THE LANDSCAPE ARCHITECT FOR THE FULL TREATMENT. If you want the total treatment from a landscape architect, he will advise you from the beginning, hopefully before your house has even been sited. His advice will be both written and oral. He aids in the preparation of surveys, develops design drawings, working drawings (such as site construction plans, grading and drainage plans, planting and irrigation plans, and related structural details), and finally specifications. In due course, he supervises the execution of his plans to assure conformity of construction to the intent of the design.

The landscape architect engaged for the total treatment will act in your behalf in selecting materials and in issuing instructions for the execution of work by contractors.

With this arrangement you just sit back, make final decisions, and pay the bills.

CHAPTER III

ᕒᕒᕒᕒᕒᕒᕒᕒᕒᕒᕒᕒᕒ

PLANS

THAT HAVE WORKED

ᕒᕒᕒᕒᕒᕒᕒᕒᕒᕒᕒᕒᕒᕒ   When a homeowner attempts any do-it-yourself project, it pays to borrow from the experience of professionals. This is especially true in low-upkeep landscaping, since you must deal with design, both pure and applied, an extensive knowledge of plant materials, and future maintenance requirements of your property.

The five plans that follow were developed by leading landscape architects and designers for places in various parts of this country. Each represents a totally different set of circumstances and owner interests. Whatever your property or climate, these plans will give you low-upkeep ideas on which to build or plant.

WILLIAMSBURG WITHOUT UPKEEP

Landscape architect William L. Koenig updated the surroundings of a fine old house, making the plan and the planting functional for present-day needs, and at the same time retaining the traditional charm of a Colonial garden. Areas paved with old bricks were introduced, reducing the amount of lawn and creating space for outdoor living. The lawn is defined in sweeping curves that simplify mowing. Brick edging strips eliminate all hand trimming of the grass. English ivy, interplanted with daffodils for spring flowers, carpets the ground around flowering trees. Background borders, carefully planned for interest in all seasons, combine deciduous shrubs with broadleafed and needle evergreens, and have a deep mulch of woodchips to discourage weeds and conserve moisture. Containers at front and service entries are filled with colorful bulbs, pansies, and primroses in spring, annuals in summer, and chrysanthemums in autumn.

19

Above: New garden for an old house: Old-brick paving extends from service entry to back of property. Planting pocket for flowering tree has a permanent cover of English ivy, with Poetaz narcissus underplanted for spring flowers. Wisteria trained on trellis next to house makes a breath-taking show when it blooms in April, and gives welcome shade for the windows in summer. The picket fence, main house, and garden storage buildings are unified by painting all in the same subtle shade of yellow.

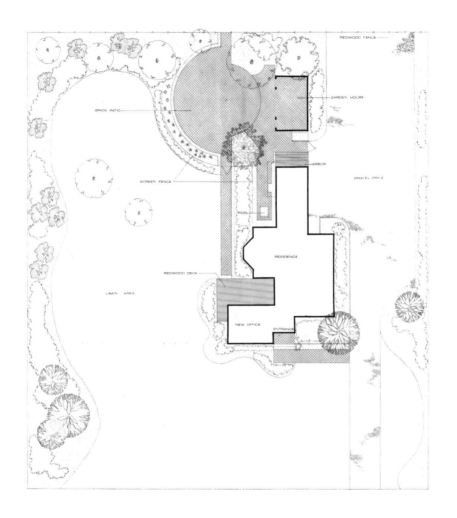

Within the plan, the following labels appear:

REDWOOD FENCE

GARDEN HOUSE

BRICK PATIO

ARBOR

GRAVEL DRIVE

SCREEN FENCE

POOL

RESIDENCE

REDWOOD DECK

LAWN AREA

NEW OFFICE

ENTRANCE

Left: Shrubbery border in background gives an ever-changing and colorful backdrop for a spacious out-door living area. What was once a carriage house has been converted to a garden work center and space for tool storage.

21

A PRIVATE WORLD IN A SMALL SPACE

A different type of landscaping changed this 85- x 100-foot lot from an area as exposed as a goldfish bowl to a secluded retreat where every square inch of space counts. Designers Goldberg and Rodler developed a master plan that could be executed in stages as the owner's budget permitted. The outdoor living room came first, with a broad expanse of brick paving for entertaining. Four existing trees provided the shade for a cool woodland retreat.

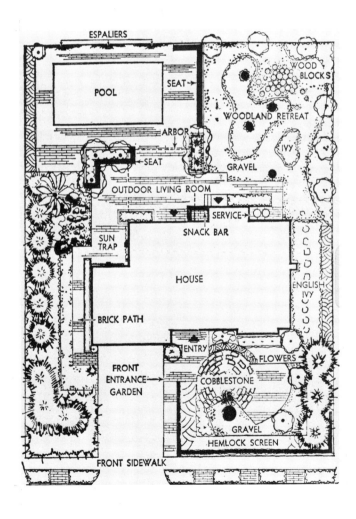

The 15- x 30-foot swimming pool was added later in the same season. Local ordinances required a high chain-link fence around the pool. This was disguised, in part, with redwood fencing, benches for seating, and a natural evergreen hedge that needs no trimming. The following year, the brick paving was extended to make a sun trap, with space for a small Japanese garden. The final work was done in the front yard with a combination of brick, cobblestone, and gravel paving that radiates from a large old shade tree. A tall, dense hemlock hedge screens this entry court from the street and reduces traffic noise. Maintenance consists of leaf raking in fall and spring, and pruning once a year.

rick-paved outdoor living room and swimming pool eliminate all grass. Fiber-lass roof over dining area filters sun and gives protection from summer showers. lowering plants in containers may be enjoyed at close range.

Four trees give an escape into the shade with a broad path of water-polished stones, natural-wood rounds as the flooring for rattan furniture, and an island of English ivy ground-cover. Rustic stockade fence gives privacy without upkeep. *Mal Gurian Assoc. photo.*

Left: Where formerly a front lawn was used only to result in time and money spent in maintenance, it is now a private entry court for more pleasant pursuits. Every trace of upkeep has vanished at the hand of a skillful landscape designer. *Mal Gurian Assoc. photo.*

Right: Untrimmed hemlock hedge screens driveway and parking area from entry court. All evergreens have a generous stone mulch which eliminates weeding and cultivating. *Mal Gurian Assoc. photo.*

A SOPHISTICATED CITY GARDEN

Whether you live in a town house or a suburban development, a garden can be a retreat from the world—a place to think or play, away from the cares of the humdrum.

Thomas Church, considered by many the father of modern American landscaping, took the miniature 16-foot front yard of a rambling San Francisco house and transformed it into a tiny island of peace and privacy. You can adapt some of his ideas to create a hideaway of your own.

Nothing deadens noise, insures privacy, and creates a sense of security like a brick wall. Paint it white and you add a feeling of spaciousness. Then scale the furniture and plantings, for aesthetics and practicality, to the limited space. Light it at night and you could be living in Camelot. This approach works in a very small property or in a private garden of a large open landscape.

Keep a jardiniere filled with colorful annuals. Pave with permanent surfaces, and take a clue from Mr. Church's treatment by using evergreen shrubs, and you have a miniature garden which is reasonably maintenance free.

Work is limited to trimming the topiaries and in a small garden that is more art than labor.

This urban garden designed by Thomas Church is partitioned into an entrance area and quiet place for eating, entertaining, or meditating. A row of trimmed plane trees screens it from second-story windows of the house across the street. *Maynard L. Parker photo.*

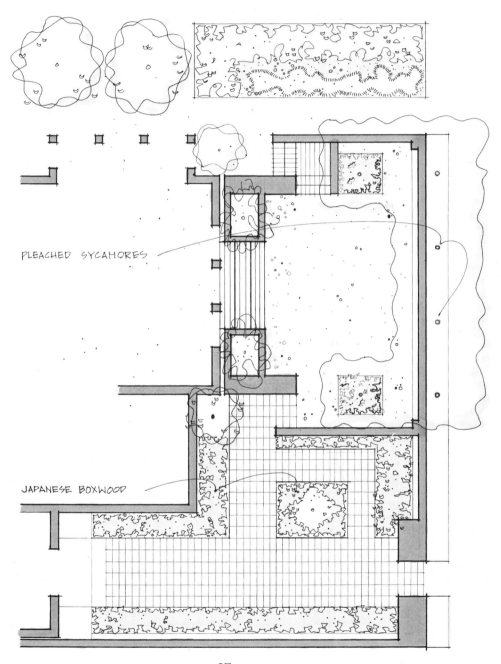

PLEACHED SYCAMORES

JAPANESE BOXWOOD

27

A LANDSCAPE FOR ENTERTAINING

Robert Zion designed this outdoor living room for a family who enjoy entertaining. The entire small area available was planned solely for dining and parties. Maintenance is limited to the pleasant tasks of training the two dwarf espaliered fruit trees, and seasonal changes of the flower containers. Three crab-apple trees flower in spring, give shade in summer, and colorful fruit in autumn. A fence for privacy and shelter from wind also hides the utility and parking space. Gravel extended from slate patio under tree (lower right in the plan) is used by owners in summer to display vacationing house plants. This plan, based on the modules used for paving, can be used as the complete, total garden on a small lot, or simply one part of a large property.

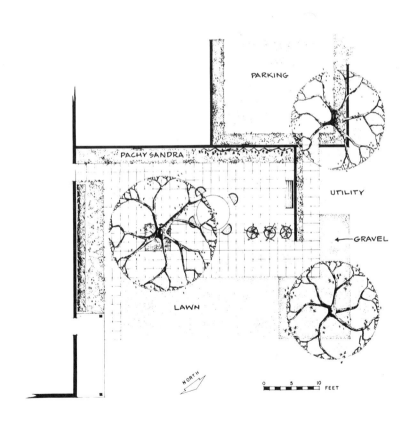

This inviting outdoor living room requires just enough maintenance to satisfy the gardener in every family. Two dwarf espaliers need light pruning two or three times each year. Containers of fall chrysanthemums are followed by spring bulbs and summer annuals. Hardy ferns grow at base of apple tree. Pachysandra covers strip of ground between patio and wall. Robert Zion, L. A. *Alexandre Georges photo.*

MAKING A LARGE PROPERTY MANAGEABLE

The terrain on Long Island, like that of the Midwest is low and flat. When Robert Zion was commissioned to landscape the grounds of a contemporary house in the heart of a New York suburb, he had to bring interest to a basically uninspired setting and at the same time keep the maintenance of a large property at a minimum. His assets were some good-sized shade trees, a clean-lined beautifully proportioned house, and a well-deserved reputation as one of the country's foremost landscape architects.

Absolute minimum of maintenance was achieved by the complete elimination of grass in favor of evergreen ground-covers of different shades and textures (ivy, pachysandra, vinca, etc.).

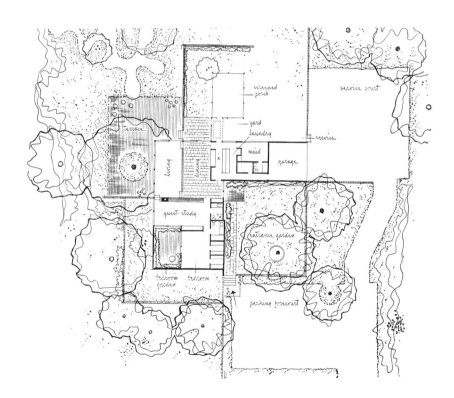

Since the ground-cover would not tolerate foot traffic, a path system through the property was a necessity. The paths would be under constant view from within the glass-walled house and Mr. Zion wanted something more interesting than conventional straight-line walkways. The free-form curved gravel paths he designed created soft fluid movement and gave a sense of levels to the landscape. Except for containers of annuals used on the terrace, flowers were restricted to spring and fall bulbs which appear year after year with almost no care. These were massed at the entrance to overwhelm the visitor.

Outside areas are designed as a series of rooms. Under Mr. Zion's expert hand, a simple parking area becomes a piazza for viewing the house and also serves as an auxiliary terrace for large parties.

Free-form gravel paths and evergreen ground-covers eliminate upkeep, relieve the flatness of the property, and at the same time soften the austere modular architecture of the house. *Mal Gurian Assoc. photo.*

Flowering trees like those in the background are used whenever possible. This sunny terrace gets additional color, without work, from containers of annuals.

The mixture of spring and fall flowering bulbs and evergreen ground-covers in a raised planting bed makes an entrance-way striking at any time of the year, with minimum care. The elm tree, necessarily left growing at its original level to preserve it, was walled around, the well creating a design feature. Lighting in the well makes the tree a piece of sculpture, equally interesting in summer and winter.

CHAPTER IV

🔳🔳🔳🔳🔳🔳🔳🔳🔳🔳🔳🔳🔳

LANDSCAPING

TO SOLVE PROBLEMS

🔳🔳🔳🔳🔳🔳🔳🔳🔳🔳🔳🔳🔳

Perfectly landscaped properties don't just happen. They must be carefully planned. Since no homeowner has an ideal site, the techniques of low-upkeep landscaping should be applied to existing problems, not only to compensate for them but also to incorporate them into a design that gives the property individuality and character. A steep slope can become a distinctive rock garden. The tiniest of back yards can extend living space, with a patio for eating and entertaining, a children's play area, and a place to store tools and equipment. The right trees and shrubs strategically placed can transform an ugly-duckling house while providing shade, wind control, privacy, and even flowers.

Whether you have a flat lot that needs interesting changes in grade, or a hilly site that needs some flat spaces, the pictures that follow can show you how to make your property more livable with less work.

What to do with a long narrow lot: Let a curved retaining wall visually shorten the length, and furnish
a second level. Mowing strip eliminates hand trimming of grass. Raised planting beds are filled with
easy-care hardy perennials. Container plants accent
and soften the ends of the steps and are displayed
on the ledge near the table and chairs. Douglas
Baylis, L. A. *Rondal Partridge photo.*

35

Privacy obtained on a small property: Evergreen trees screen the house in all seasons. Locusts cast lacy, light shade in summer. Bricked entry court, free-form paths of stone mulch, and islands of English ivy reduce the lawn area. Japanese lantern glows pleasantly at night from lighted candle inside. Landscaping by Goldberg and Rodler. *Mal Gurian Assoc. photo.*

One small garden that solves big problems: 8-foot wooden fence gives privacy and shelter from wind, at the same time hiding an unpleasant view. Deck extends interior space into the outdoor living area and reduces the amount of lawn upkeep. Only a few trees and shrubs are needed for all-year color, with pots of flowers added in season. *Western Wood Products Association photo.*

Slatted wood fence stops the eye but not the air. Large flowering cherry tree gives a bouquet of bloom in spring with shade in summer for a bed of hardy ferns, mulched with pebbles to avoid weeding. *Western Wood Products Association photo.*

With the neighbor's house less than **40** feet away, privacy is achieved with bamboo screening framed by dark-stained wood that needs no upkeep. Precast concrete patio blocks serve as walk leading from wood deck. Firbark chips are used as mulch, in combination with *Vinca minor* as ground-cover.

An outdoor living space when there is no back yard?
Landscape architect Robert Zion solved the problem
by building a brick wall along front of the property.
Courtyard requires virtually no upkeep. Containers
of annual flowers at entry need only planting in
spring, watering in dry weather, and keeping spent
flowers removed. Evergreen espaliers on the walls
are pruned occasionally as needed.

A spacious out-of-doors room has been created on a
hilly site by using a brick retaining wall to level
ground for the slate-paved patio and by cantilevering a redwood deck with built-in seating. Landscaping by Goldberg and Rodler. *Mal Gurian Assoc.
photo.*

41

To reduce the lawn area on a large property: Plant trees and shrubs in stone-mulched islands, with walkways, steps, and living areas paved in bricks and slate. English ivy ground-cover, yew hedge, and shrubbery plantings of andromeda and rhododendron stay green all year. The shrubs also flower in spring. For color near chairs and lounges, use pots of impatiens and caladiums. Landscaping by Goldberg and Rodler. *Mal Gurian Assoc. photo.*

By extending a raised deck from small existing brick patio, owners successfully gained space for outdoor living, at the same time reducing lawn care. Slightly raised deck gives interest to otherwise flat site. Wooden screen at right hides utility area and air-conditioning condenser. Landscaping by Goldberg and Rodler. *Mal Gurian Assoc. photo.*

The owners once struggled to maintain a lawn in this tiny city garden. Now they have a charming formal garden that requires no demanding upkeep. Dwarf boxwood outlines the brick-edged beds. In sunny center areas, geraniums give summer color. Tulips and hyacinths planted in fall (at the end of geranium season) give spring flowers. A collection of tuberous-rooted begonias grows in the more shaded area along wall, preceded in spring by daffodils that come up without care, year after year. *George Taloumis photo.*

Brilliant flower borders are enhanced by healthy turf. To achieve the effect without a sweep of lawn, brick paths and mowing strips may be used to reduce the maintenance. *George Taloumis photo.*

45

A steep bank is no place for grass. Here California landscape architect Lawrence Halprin used as many of the existing native trees and shrubs as possible to please the eye and prevent erosion. Outcroppings of stone were carefully arranged to look natural. Planting pockets were filled with low-growing perennials that give flowers from earliest spring until fall. *Morley Baer photo.*

For an atrium open to the sky, and always on view from inside the house, Robert Zion used dark stone chips and brick for the surface, with an edging ground-cover of ajuga. Each year the owner changes the flowers. Tulips or daffodils are fall-planted for spring. Dwarf petunias, French marigolds, and Button zinnias have all been used for bright summer color. Even in dormancy, the espaliered grapevine makes an interesting tracery on the wall.

47

Instead of fencing a large property, privacy for outdoor living is achieved with a raised planting bed
that is easy to cultivate and serves in a practical way
as a well for the shade tree. *Maynard L. Parker
photo.*

Wind control in a treeless area is gained from curved redwood screen, made up of a series of straight sections tangential to an arc. The bench is formed by curved redwood 2 x 4's on edge. Landscape design by Royston, Hanamoto and Mayes. *Phil Palmer photo.*

CHAPTER V

ᘓᘓᘓᘓᘓᘓᘓᘓᘓᘓᘓᘓᘓ

TREES:

EVERY HOME NEEDS THEM

ᘓᘓᘓᘓᘓᘓᘓᘓᘓᘓᘓᘓ Every property must have at least one shade tree, more if there is room, and flowering trees too as space permits, but select no tree that is a maintenance trap. Avoid any tree known to be disease-prone (American elm), insect-ridden (black-locust), or having shallow wide-spreading roots (cottonwood). Also beware of trees with large, brittle branches that may snap in a wind storm (silver maple), kinds that send suckers far out into lawn and garden areas (some poplars), and any with smelly blossoms (female poplar, male ailanthus), or littering fruit (red mulberry).

When you plant a tree, you are planting shade, either dense as from a sycamore, or light and open, as from a honey-locust. You are also planting shape, background, and color—from bark, leaves, flowers, and possibly fruit.

Select trees for screening, to shut off an unsightly view, to afford privacy from neighbors, or to muffle street noise. Trees can mask or complement the stark lines of buildings. Trees along a street give a feeling of welcome.

To select the tree that will give maximum effect with minimum effort, consider: (1) reliable winter hardiness; (2) form suited to use; (3) mature size, including rate of growth; (4) any undesirable characteristics; and (5) availability.

1. HARDINESS. This pertains to climate, soil, moisture, heat, and cold. For example, the European mountain-ash thrives in northern climates but is short-lived in the South. The ginkgo and the London plane-tree prosper even in air-polluted city gardens and along city streets. The sugar maple expires in cities; it needs fresh air. For easy maintenance, select trees *known* to thrive in

The Moraine locust is an excellent shade tree, growing eventually to 75 feet. It casts light shade, requires little or no leaf raking in autumn, and also bears no thorns or seedpods. *Siebenthaler photo.*

The Siberian elm—usually called "Chinese"—is known botanically as *Ulmus pumila*. It is a fast-growing shade tree with a spreading head. The leaves turn yellow in autumn, and most blow away after frost, requiring little or no raking. *U.S. Forest Service photo.*

your climate. Take a look at what is growing well on your neighbors' places. Obviously, some watering, feeding, pruning, and spraying may be needed but not to the point of being a weekly or monthly chore.

2. FORM DEPENDS ON FUNCTION. A broad-spreading shade tree, like the sugar maple, is fine in the open spaces of a park or large yard, but not along a driveway, or dripping branches over the front door. Slim upright trees, such as Lombardy poplar, are fine for screening or to line a drive, but one won't function well to shade an outdoor-living area, and it is certainly not a tree to nourish for ten years with the hope of eventually enjoying a picnic lunch beneath it.

Tree people say there are six basic shapes: *columnar* (Lombardy poplar), *oval* (horse-chestnut, red ash), *pyramidal* (pin oak, yellow-wood), *round* (catalpa, willow oak), *spreading/horizontal* (Amur cork-tree, weeping willow, and *vase* (hybrid elm). Sometimes a seventh category is suggested, *weeping* (willow). This sounds perfectly sensible on paper, but when you go to the nursery, the basic shapes may not be so obvious because specimens there are immature. Ask your nurseryman and read catalog descriptions carefully for information about the two-dimensional shape of the tree you are considering.

3. SIZE is a consideration everyone takes seriously—at least at first. The temptation is to fall in love with an appealing young specimen at the nursery—like a St. Bernard puppy in a pet shop—and take it home, regardless of its expected size at maturity. That symmetrical Norway spruce at the nursery, only 6 feet tall, appears ideal for planting near the entry. But it will grow to 70 feet, with a spread of 40 feet.

When you plant two or more trees of the same kind, the general rule for spacing is at a distance equal to 75 percent of height. For example, trees expected to grow 20 feet tall should be planted 15 feet apart.

Also to be considered is a tree's expected growth rate under normal conditions. Sometimes a potentially large tree grows so slowly that it is still a good choice. For example, a tulip-tree may grow to 100 feet, but this takes a hundred years. You may elect to plant the tulip-tree for your own enjoyment and let future genera-

Paul's Scarlet hawthorn (Crataegus) is a small tree, covered with pink flowers in the spring and clusters of red berries in autumn. The Wayside Gardens Co. photo.

tions worry about its ultimate size. It takes a ginkgo fifteen to twenty years to make a real show.

CAREFREE DECIDUOUS TREES FOR SHADE

The heights given below merely indicate the average height in cultivation about 25 to 30 years after planting. Of course, individual specimens of the larger trees may continue to grow, under favorable conditions, for many decades and will reach 100 to 140 feet by the time your grandchildren are grown. Such are the bur oak, sugar maple, tulip-tree, white ash, and white oak. Moderately quick-growing trees have one asterisk (*), and fast-growing trees have two (**).

American Linden, *Tilia americana*, 50 ft., heavy shade, fragrant blossoms in late June, slow-growing.

American Sycamore, *Platanus occidentalis*, 50 ft., heavy shade, often holds its leaves until late fall, mottled bark, magnificent when large.**

Amur Cork-tree, *Phellodendron amurense*, 40 ft., wide-spreading top, compound leaves, black berries, good in dry soils.*

Box-elder, *Acer negundo*, 40 ft., open airy growth, often several main trunks, very hardy.**

Buisman Hybrid Elm, *Ulmus* 'Christine Buisman', 40 ft., resistant to Dutch elm disease.*

Bur Oak, *Quercus macrocarpa*, 50 ft., needs space to develop superbly, slow-growing.

Chinese Chestnut, *Castanea mollissima*, 50 ft., good shade, edible nuts after ten years, slow-growing.

Chinese Elm, *see* Siberian Elm.

Cutleaf Weeping Birch, *Betula pendula gracilis*, 40 ft., white bark, exotic look, light shade.*

European Ash, *Fraxinus excelsior*, 50 ft., good shade.*

European Beech, *Fagus sylvatica*, 50 ft., smooth pale-gray bark, low branches, glossy leaves.*

European Birch, *Betula pendula*, 40 ft., white bark, very graceful; light shade.*

European Hornbeam, *Carpinus betulus*, 50 ft., broad-pyramidal form, densely foliaged, slow-growing.

Ginkgo, *Ginkgo triloba*, 40 ft., stiff-looking and often odd-shaped when young, beautiful in 15 years, brassy late-autumn foliage, immune to all pests.**

Green Ash, *Fraxinus pennsylvanica lanceolata,* 50 ft., stately form, solid shade.**

Hackberry, *Celtis occidentalis,* 50 ft., elmlike leaves, branching crown, open shade.**

Horse-chestnut, *Aesculus hippocastanum,* 50 ft., large compound leaves, smooth bark, vigorous form with pendent limbs when mature, candelabra blossoms, dense shade.**

Kentucky Coffee-tree, *Gymnocladus dioica,* 40 ft., rounded, open form, large leaves.*

Little-leaf Linden, *Tilia cordata,* 40 ft., densely foliaged, graceful branches, fragrant flowers in June, heavy shade.

Locust, *Robinia pseudoacacia,* 50 ft., high open form, cool blue-green foliage, limbs brittle when old (avoid planting near walks and drives).**

Lombardy Poplar, *Populus nigra italica,* 50 ft., narrow-columned, short-lived. Leaves always in motion.**

Modesto Ash, *Fraxinus velutina glauca,* 20 ft., rounded form, drought-resistant, good in small areas.**

Moraine Locust, *Gleditsia triacanthos,* 50 ft., open, graceful, airy form, grass grows underneath, light shade.**

Norway Maple, *Acer platanoides,* 50 ft., good shade and fall coloring.**

Pagoda-tree, *Sophora japonica,* 40 ft., spreading crown, delicate but dense foliage, clustered flowers in August on mature trees.*

Pin Oak, *Quercus palustris,* 50 ft., densely foliaged, downward-slanted limbs, pyramidal effect.*

Red Maple, *Acer rubrum,* 50 ft., small leaves for a maple but good shade, shallow-rooting, leaves color in fall.**

Red Oak, *Quercus borealis,* 40 ft., rounded form, crimson autumn color.*

Malus floribunda is one of the showiest
of many flowering crab-apples. Most
species and varieties form small trees
that blossom profusely in late April to
early May and bear red fruits in late
summer and fall. *The Wayside Gardens
Co. photo.*

57

Prunus serrulata sargentii is one of the hardiest and most beautiful of the Japanese Flowering cherries. It grows to about 20 feet high, and blooms in early spring. *Paul E. Genereux photo.*

River Birch, *Betula nigra*, 50 ft., upright form with branching trunk, ragged bark.**

Russian Olive, *Elaeagnus angustifolia*, 20 ft., silvery foliage, stands drought, very hardy.**

Sassafras, *Sassafras albidum*, 40 ft., irregular open form, interesting leaves color reddish in fall.*

Scarlet Oak, *Quercus coccinea*, 40 ft., irregular form, brilliant autumn color, slow-growing.

Shagbark Hickory, *Carya ovata*, 50 ft., rugged, picturesque form, many branched and tall-oval in form, bark smooth on young trees, shaggy-plated on older ones, needs care in transplanting and moist soil.**

Siberian Elm, *Ulmus pumila*, 40 ft., spreading form, good autumn foliage. Very hardy.**

Sugar Maple, *Acer saccharum*, 50 ft., dense crown of foliage turning orange, yellow, and red in fall. Rather slow-growing, handsome.

Sweet Gum, *Liquidambar styraciflua*, 50 ft., star-shaped leaves, wine-red autumn color, moist soil.*

Tulip-tree, *Liriodendron tulipifera*, 50 ft., tall straight trunk, beautiful leaves, orange-green flowers in June, yellow autumn color.**

Weeping Willow, *Salix babylonica*, 40 ft., long pendent flexible branchlets, lower ones touching the ground.**

White Ash, *Fraxinus americana*, 50 ft., large compound leaves, open growth, stately when fully grown.*

White Oak, *Quercus alba*, 50 ft., spreading form, vigorous noble look, red leaves in fall, slow-growing.

Willow Oak, *Quercus phellos*, 40 ft., slender, light-green leaves, more airy and open effect than other oaks, hardy to lower New England.*

Yellow-wood, *Cladrastis lutea*, 30 ft., low-branching.*

CAREFREE FLOWERING TREES

Very few showy flowering trees grow to more than 25 feet tall, and many are nearly as wide as high. In this list the specified heights are the ultimate height, which most will attain in fifteen to twenty years. Exceptions are the empress-tree, which may take longer to reach 40 feet and may then, in a fortunate situation, go on well beyond that; and the saucer magnolia, which may develop into a fairly large tree in time. Many flowering trees, also, branch fairly close to the ground, and have the effect of large shrubs, so that they can be used in combinations, where there is space, or as isolated specimens.

American Redbud, *Cercis canadensis,* 15 ft. Pink pea-flowers all along branches in May.

Bechtel's Crab Apple, *Malus ioensis plena,* 20 ft. Double pale-pink flowers in profusion in May.

Empress-tree, *Pawlownia tomentosa,* 40 ft. Hardy to lower New York State. Large panicles of violet flowers before the leaves.

English Hawthorn, *Crataegus oxyacantha,* 15 ft. White fragrant flowers in large clusters. Scarlet berries. Also a pink-flowered form.

European Mountain-ash, *Sorbus aucuparia,* 25 ft. White flowers in spring. Red berries in summer and fall.

Flowering Cherries, *Prunus serrulata,* 20 ft. Wealth of fragrant white flowers just before the leaves. A fine variety is known as *P. sargentii.*

Prunus sieboldii, 25 ft. Dangling clusters of pink flowers. A fine lawn specimen.

Prunus subhirtella pendula, 25 ft. Fountain of pink flowers in spring.

Prunus yedoensis, 30 ft. Fast-growing, single white or palest pink flowers.

Flowering Dogwood, *Cornus florida,* 30 ft. Familiar, and one of the outstanding American trees.

Flowering Peach, *Prunus persica* varieties, 10 ft. White, pink, or red flowers in May.

Build a patio around a shade tree if you want protection from noonday sun. To keep the tree in good condition, circle it with a stone-mulched island so that water and air can reach the roots. Landscaping by Goldberg and Rodler. *Mal Gurian Assoc. photo.*

Flowering Plum, *Prunus blireiana,* 20 ft. Rose-colored double flowers in May, purple-tinged leaves.

Prunus pissardi, 20 ft. Deep-pink flowers, plum-colored leaves. Also a white-flowered form.

Franklinia, *Gordonia alatamaha,* 20 ft. Hardy to Massachusetts. Large white flowers in autumn.

Fringe-tree, *Chionanthus virginica,* 20 ft. Hardy to lower New York State.

Goldenchain, *Laburnum vossei,* 25 ft. Pendent racemes of yellow pea-flowers in May.

The Black Hills spruce (*Picea glauca densata*) is a slow-growing evergreen tree that thrives in a sunny place in almost any soil, but it does prefer cool summer weather. *U.S. Forest Service photo.*

Goldenrain-tree, *Koelreuteria paniculata,* 30 ft. Panicles of bloom in midsummer.

Hopa Crab Apple, *Malus hopa,* 25 ft. Spectacular show of brilliant pink flowers in May.

Japanese Crab Apple, *Malus sieboldii,* 15 ft. Slender habit, blush-pink flowers.

> *Malus floribunda,* 20 ft. Buds carmine, opening to pink flowers, then white. Very showy.

Japanese Dogwood, *Cornus kousa,* 20 ft. Blooms later than flowering dogwood. Leaves scarlet in autumn.

Mimosa, *see* Silk-tree.

Red Horse-chestnut, *Aesculus carnea,* 40 ft. Flowers flesh-color to scarlet in June.

Sargent's Crab Apple, *Malus sargentii,* 6 ft. Shrublike; white flowers, red fruits.

Saucer Magnolia, *Magnolia soulangeana,* 30 ft. White, pink, and rose-colored flowers in different varieties.

Shadblow, *Amelanchier grandiflora,* 25 ft. Snow-white flowers in spring.

Siberian Crab Apple, *Malus baccata,* 25 ft. White flowers in May. Fruits yellow or red.

Silk-tree, *Albizzia julibrissin,* 30 ft. Airy foliage. Pink flowers like erect tassels in summer. May winterkill north of Philadelphia.

Silverbell, *Halesia monticola,* 30 ft. Profuse white flowers in late May. Rich moist soil.

Star Magnolia, *Magnolia stellata,* 15 ft. White flowers in early spring.

Tree Lilac, *Syringa japonica,* 25 ft. Large trusses of white flowers in June. Wide-branching.

Washington Hawthorn, *Crataegus cordata*, 20 ft. Flowers in late spring. Fall berries. Leaves turn red in autumn.

There are other fine species and hybrids of crab apples, cherries, hawthorns, and plums. Consult the catalogs of leading nurseries. In the northernmost parts of the country the crab apples are hardier than the cherries and plums.

CAREFREE EVERGREEN TREES

American Arborvitae, *Thuja occidentalis*, to 60 ft. but many much lower-growing forms of various shapes. Dense foliage, scale-like leaves. Slow-growing.

American Holly, *Ilex opaca*, to 40 ft. Familiar glossy leaves. Male and female trees needed to produce berries. May require spraying for leaf miners.

Austrian Pine, *Pinus nigra*, to 60 ft. Dark needles, open growth. Fine for background. Hardy.

Black Hills Spruce, *Picea glauca densata*, to 40 ft. Slow-growing, compact, symmetrical.

Cedar of Lebanon, *Cedrus libani*, to 60 ft. Blue-green foliage. Not hardy north of New York City except along the coast.

Colorado Spruce, *Picea pungens*, to 40 ft. Blue-green foliage. Many varieties, very hardy.

Douglas-fir, *Pseudotsuga taxifolia*, to 40 ft. (eventually a giant in nature). Var. *glauca* the best in northern and eastern gardens.

Eastern Hemlock, *Tsuga canadensis*, to 60 ft. Graceful, soft-foliaged. Needs lime soil.

English Holly, *Ilex aquifolium*, 20 ft. Perhaps more beautiful than American holly, but not reliably hardy north of Philadelphia. Slow-growing. May require spraying for leaf miners.

Hinoki False-cypress, *Chamaecyparis obtusa*, to 20 ft. Foliage flat and frond-like, drooping. Many varieties.

The White, or Colorado, fir (*Abies concolor*) has fine-textured blue-green needles. The small, tapered cones grow upright on the branches. Needs a sunny place, preferably with moist soil. *U.S. Forest Service photo.*

Norway or Red Pine, *Pinus resinosa,* 60 ft. One of the hardiest and best large pines. Open, branching shape.

Norway Spruce, *Picea abies,* to 40 ft. Many forms. Generally dense, pyramidal, light-green foliage effect. Pendent cones.

Scotch Pine, *Pinus sylvestris,* to 30 ft. Blue-green foliage. Picturesque habit.

White or Colorado Fir, *Abies concolor,* to 40 ft. Many forms. Soft-
green color effect.

White Pine, *Pinus strobus,* to 60 ft. Majestic tree, branches beautifully spaced. When older, dark foliage.

4. UNDESIRABLE TRAITS VARY IN IMPORTANCE.   Some make a
tree completely undesirable for planting; others may be tolerable.
The American elm is at present a poor choice. Thornless honey-
locust is subject to attack by the mimosa webworm—as is the
mimosa (silk-tree) itself—and this needs annual spraying. Mulberry species and the female ginkgo have objectionable fruit;
plant the fruitless variety of white mulberry and male ginkgo.
More tolerable are the traits of oaks, hickories, horse-chestnuts,
and crab apples that drop fruit over lawn or terrace—fruits attractive to children who are always tempted to use them as missiles.
The stickery-sphere seed pods dropped on the lawn by sweet
gum are a nuisance, but easily managed by an annual rake-up in
the spring and completely offset by the glorious coloration of the
autumn foliage.

Poplars, silk-trees, maples, and elms readily seed into lawns and
flower beds. But this is really no problem unless the seedlings are
allowed to grow for a season or two; then they are hard to uproot
and a real time-consumer. Some trees have hungry surface roots
that rob the soil of all moisture, making it impossible to grow a
decent lawn there, or flowers: maples, for example. Roots also may
crack nearby pavement. Some trees have vigorous roots that seek
out sewer lines and clog them—red and silver maples, elms, and
willows.

5. AVAILABILITY.   Narrow your list. Decide exactly what tree is
your choice—and the best tree for the location. Then go after it.
If it is not available at a local nursery, shop by mail. There is no
reason to accept any substitute, unless you can honestly say that
after further consideration it is in reality a better choice.

The Prostrate or Creeping junipers (a form of *Juniperus horizontalis* is shown) make excellent ground-covers in rocky places or along a steep bank where mowing would be difficult or impossible. *Kassler Studios photo*.

PLANTING

If you have selected the right trees and planned for them in your design, minimum upkeep should be your reward. Before you rush out with the loaf of bread and jug of wine, take time to plant them properly.

The one major rule about tree planting is to dig a large hole. If the tree is balled and burlapped, dig a hole 2 feet wider than the rootball. Depth—check ring around the trunk to determine the original soil line—and plant to the same level.

If the soil is poor, dig an even wider and deeper hole, replacing a quantity of the poor soil with best possible topsoil.

Before adding soil around the rootball, add stakes or guy post. If the trunk is less than 3 inches in diameter, use one or two 6-foot poles set vertically next to the rootball. Fasten the trunk to the poles with loops of wire enclosed in a section of garden hose (to protect bark). For a trunk larger than 3 inches in diameter, use three guy wires, hose-covered, around the trunk about halfway up. Stake one guy wire to the ground in the direction of the prevailing wind, the other two placed to form an equilateral triangle.

After the stakes or guy wires are in place, fill in topsoil, being sure tree is positioned in a straight vertical position. Water well. After soil settles, add more to level off. Wrap trunk with burlap or creped Kraft paper to prevent sunscald. Start wrapping at top; work down. Tie with stout cord knotting about every 18 inches. Remove after two years, or when it begins to fall away.

How to compensate if you planted a tree without digging a large hole to begin with? You will have to water more frequently, in combination with more fertilizer, than for a tree well-planted to begin with. Soil that is heavily compacted is often either so dry that roots cannot prosper in it, or so poorly drained that water stands and suffocates the roots. If dryness is the problem, make a basin around the trunk that will hold water and fill it often to keep the soil evenly moist. If the soil is too wet, gently mound it higher at the trunk than the surrounding area so that rain will run off from the tree, not be caught and held around it.

TREES NEED FERTILIZER

Feeding at the right time in the right amounts will give you healthy, strong trees that grow at a satisfying rate. Once a year is sufficient. If you start a new tree with a large hole and fill in around it with good topsoil, no feeding will be needed the first year. After that, feed annually, in spring. Measure the trunk 3 feet above ground. Allow 2 pounds of 5-10-5 for each inch of diameter. A one-pound coffee can holds about 2 pounds of fertilizer. Use soil auger, crowbar, or posthole digger. Make holes 15 to 24 inches deep and 18 to 24 inches apart around dripline of the tree (this is the area underneath the longest branches).

Distribute fertilizer equally in the holes. Fill back-up with soil made by mixing equal parts soil and sand; this accepts moisture readily.

Trees should be deeply watered frequently during the first two seasons after planting. An automatic watering system will help here. Once established, trees can survive long periods of drought. City trees get very little water because large paved areas are so planned that moisture drains away quickly before it can seep underneath. They adjust. Lawn trees compete with grass and other plants nearby. At first, it is necessary to let water soak slowly for several hours around each tree. Later, in times of severe drought, if there is a water shortage, water the trees first; then choice shrubbery; last of all herbaceous flowers which by comparison in the final analysis are expendable. It takes years to grow a tree; only a season or two to grow a flower garden.

Mulching helps conserve moisture around a tree and reduces maintenance—no need to hand trim after mowing the grass and no danger of scruffing the bark with passes from the mower. Both points are important. Trees are naturally mulched in the forest by layers of leaves that fall and lie year after year gradually decomposing. Not possible in cultivated areas. So, add a mulch of pine bark, tanbark, ground corncobs, redwood bark, peanut hulls, or pebbles. General rule: Area to mulch beneath a tree should be twelve times diameter of the trunk. A tree 1 inch in diameter will need a mulch area a foot in diameter. A tree with a 5-inch trunk will need a mulch area 5 feet in diameter.

Pruning is routine. If you have chosen the right tree, it is also minimal. Winter is a good time to check overall structure. After leafing-out of tree, it is easier to find dead, dying, or unsightly parts. Pruning will help improve the appearance. Direct the growth and avoid major surgery later. Once-a-year pruning will make it easy to get rid of undesirable branches and shoots while they are still small—no sawing, only simple cutting with a pair of shears.

When pruning is in order, look for: dead, dying, or unsightly tree parts. Sprouts growing at or near base of trunk. Branches growing toward center of tree. Crossed branches. (Crossed branches rub together; disease and decay fungi enter through abraded parts.) V crotches: If possible remove one branch; v's split easily in wind, ice, and snow storms. Multiple leaders: If tree should have one to develop typical shape, remove all but one leader. Nuisance growth: Remove branches headed toward utility wires. Those that shade tree lights. That block view of street (potential traffic hazard, for example). That may screen a desirable view. Remove branches that stop breezes. Remove lower limbs that shade lawn too much or make walking underneath hazardous.

When you prune, don't leave stubs. They die back, tend to rot, and become a breeding place for dangerous fungi. Small cuts heal quickly. Large cuts—anything more than 1 inch in diameter—need treatment with antiseptic tree dressing to prevent the entrance of decay-disease while wound heals.

ᴙᴙᴙᴙᴙᴙᴙᴙᴙᴙᴙᴙᴙ

SHRUBS:

LOTS OF THEM

ᴙᴙᴙᴙᴙᴙᴙᴙᴙᴙᴙᴙᴙᴙ Plant shrubs wherever you want year-round interest—flowers, foliage, berries, and colorful bark—and no demanding upkeep. Evergreen and deciduous shrubs come in all sizes and shapes for plantings in sun or shade, in moist or dry soil, and in all climates. Depend on them for screening, dense and impenetrable or filtered and illusionary, and for hedging, low and formal or tall and billowy.

With shrubs, there is no need to have a maintenance problem. Apply a thick mulch around them to avoid weeding and cultivating. If you can't prune and trim annually, try for once every other year.

A common mistake with shrubs is to plant one in a space that is too small. Multiply this by planting a whole bed of shrubs poorly scaled to the space, and you will have a problem that grows worse every year. More and more pruning will be needed, until finally you give in and let the shrubbery take over, literally blocking out the doors and windows of your home.

Another maintenance trap with shrubs is to spot them all around the lawn and garden, thus necessitating additional trimming, and tedious mowing around. Better to group shrubs—even if you have only a few—in complete and well-designed beds than to scatter them all over the yard.

Different kinds of shrubs can be interplanted in a pleasing way so that foliage blends or contrasts, textures complement, and flowers come in and out of bloom in an ever-changing picture. Another approach is to mass shrubs of one kind, lilacs for example. Within this planting there will be early-, midseason-, and late-blooming varieties. The same can be done with rhododendrons and azaleas.

71

SHRUBS FOR ALL SEASONS

If it is important that you have flowers over a long season, with plenty to cut for bouquets, especially some with long stems for large arrangements, flowering shrubs are the answer. Your display can start with witch-hazels that bloom in the first spring weather—which may come in a January thaw in your area—and finish with witch-hazels that bloom in October and November. For fall and winter there are many shrubs with bright berries, and the red-twig dogwood has colorful bark.

For entrance plantings on close view around the year, ever-greens are the obvious choice. Selected with care, tailored and neat, these will prove a constant joy. To avoid maintenance, clearly delineate the bed design with a brick mowing strip or a retaining wall. Mulch the surface with wood chips or pebbles. This kind of reserve keeps the entry area looking well-groomed with little or no upkeep. For seasonal flowers, use a few well-placed containers.

Shrubs properly planted and at the right time require the least maintenance. Plan first. If you wait to decide what you want until you go to a local nursery, you will likely be tempted to buy some of everything that appeals to you. If the assortment turns into a low-upkeep planting at home, you will have worked a modern-day miracle. The miracle happens only when you plan it carefully. And this is a great pastime for winter—or a relaxed summer day when you can spread your catalogs and papers on a shaded table under a tree, or maybe in an air-conditioned room. The idea is to do the planning when planting time is yet to be. Try to locate the right shrubs in the right place at the beginning. If you have to move a shrub later to a better position, don't hesi-tate to transplant, but it's work you should try to avoid.

Shrubs are available at local garden centers as container-grown plants (usually in cans or plastic pots), large specimens some-times balled-and-burlapped, and early in spring there may be bare-root deciduous varieties. By mail most shrubs come bare-root only in early spring for immediate planting. More and more shrubs are displayed in garden centers as container-grown plants that can be seen and selected—and planted—any time the weather lets you work outdoors. This permits landscape work to proceed over a long season, instead of being limited to a few too-short

A bed of broadleaf evergreens, underplanted with pachysandra and mulched with wood chips, follows the serpentine curve of this patio, giving all-year foliage near the house, and a wave of flowers in spring and early summer from mountain-laurel, andromeda, azalea, and rhododendron. Shrubbery border at property line includes deciduous types that bloom variously from earliest spring to late summer, and needle evergreens that give color and privacy in all seasons. Arthur Edwin Bye, Jr., L. A. *Gottscho-Schleisner photo.*

Tall shade trees, trimmed high and open, permit dappled sunlight to reach this outdoor living area, thereby sustaining a few shrubs selected for year-round interest. Mentor barberry serves as a semi-evergreen, unclipped hedge. Stone-mulched beds are planted with dwarf Mugho pine, prostrate junipers, and English ivy. Mountain-laurel and rhododendrons give flowers in May and June. Landscaping by Goldberg and Rodler. *Mal Gurian Assoc. photo.*

weeks in spring, and again for a too-short period in early fall.

The lists below first group deciduous shrubs according to flowering season, with mature heights specified, followed by a selection of kinds for berries, and finally plants to consider among the broadleaf and needle leaf evergreens. From these lists, you will see that the range of choice is wide in all types and sizes. You can get an initial acquaintance with any of them in nursery catalogs, but the better way is to see them personally in a nursery, arboretum, or in neighbors' gardens.

EASY DECIDUOUS FLOWERING SHRUBS

EARLY SPRING

Cornelian-cherry, *Cornus mas,* 15 ft.
Flowering Quince, *Chaenomeles lagenaria,* 3 to 8 ft.
Forsythia, *Forsythia spectabilis* and hybrids, 10 ft.
Pussy Willow, *Salix discolor* and S. *viminalis,* 20 ft.

MID-SPRING

Azalea, *Azalea mollis* strain, many hybrids, 2 to 5 ft.
Bridal-wreath, *Spiraea prunifolia,* 6 ft.
Bush Honeysuckle, *Lonicera tatarica,* 8 ft.
Deutzia, various hybrids, 3 ft.
Flowering Almond, *Prunus glandulosa,* 4 ft.
French Lilac, *Syringa lemoinei* hybrids, 8 to 12 ft.
Jetbead, *Rhodotypos tetrapetala,* 5 ft.
Persian Lilac, *Syringa persica,* 6 ft.
Van Houtte's Spiraea, *Spiraea vanhouttei,* 6 ft.

LATE SPRING

Beauty-bush, *Kolkwitzia amabilis,* 8 ft.
Double-file Viburnum, *Viburnum tomentosum mariesi,* 7 ft.
Fragrant Snowball, *Viburnum carlcephalum,* 6 ft.
Japanese Snowball, *Viburnum tomentosum sterile,* 10 ft.
Kerria, *Kerria japonica pleniflora,* 8 ft.
Mock-orange, *Philadelphus* species and vars., 10 ft.
Red Spiraea, *Spiraea japonica coccinea,* 3 ft.
Strawberry-shrub, *Calycanthus floridus,* 6 ft.
Weigela, *Weigela florida* and hybrids, 8 ft.

MIDSUMMER

Abelia, *Abelia grandiflora,* 4 ft.
Beauty-berry, *Callicarpa giraldiana,* 8 ft.
Buddleia, *Buddleia davidi* and hybrids, 8 ft.
French Tamarix, *Tamarix gallica* and hybrids, 8 ft. Hardy to
    southern New England.
Hypericum, *Hypericum* 'Hidcote,' 3 ft., lower in cold areas.

Potentilla, *Potentilla fruticosa,* 2 ft.
Smoke-tree, *Cotinus coggygria,* 12 ft.

LATE SUMMER—EARLY FALL

Blue-mist Flower, *Caryopteris mastacanthus,* 3 ft. Often dies to
    the ground in Northeast, comes up every spring.
Chaste-tree, *Vitex agnus-castus,* 10 ft.
Peegee Hydrangea, *Hydrangea paniculata grandiflora,* 10 ft.
Rose-of-Sharon, *Hibiscus syriacus,* 8 ft.

SHRUBS AND LOW TREES WITH FALL AND WINTER BERRIES

Barberries   Hawthorns
Beauty-berry   Holly
Cornelian-cherry   Jetbead
Cotoneasters   Mountain-ash
Crab Apples   Rugosa Roses
Dogwood (also the red-twig   Snowberry
    Dogwood for winter bark)   Viburnums

DWARF BROADLEAF EVERGREENS
(under 4 feet)

Andromeda, *Pieris floribunda.*

Barberry, *Berberis julianae* and *B. mentorensis* hold their leaves
    until mid-winter. Other evergreen kinds not reliably hardy
    north of Washington, D.C.

Boxwood, Littleleaf, *Buxus microphylla.* Hardy to lower New York
    and Connecticut.

Euonymus, *Euonymus fortunei vegetus.*

Holly-grape, *Mahonia aquifolium.*

Holly, Short-leaved, *Ilex convexa.*

Leucothoe, Drooping, *Leucothoe catesbaei.* North of New York
    City best in sheltered situation.

Night-lighted forsythia makes a dramatic picture from living-room windows, with naturalized daffodils blooming at the same time. Forsythia branches pruned in late winter can be forced into early bloom indoors in a deep container of water. Otherwise, wait to prune until after flowering. *General Electric photo.*

Rhododendron, *Rhododendron carolinianum.*

Rock-spray, *Cotoneaster divaricata* and *C. horizontalis,* low, trailing.

MEDIUM-HEIGHT BROADLEAF EVERGREENS
(5 to 10 feet)

Andromeda, *Pieris japonica.*

Euonymus, *Euonymus patens,* hardy in New England. *E. japonicus* larger, hardy to Philadelphia.

Evergreen shrubs give seclusion to this little graveled terrace. Hardy candytuft (*Iberis sempervirens*) is the low hedging material (seldom so effectively used), with juniper in the background, and dwarf yews accenting entry. All are kept in shape by an annual clipping. Wood chips are used to mulch shaded areas where grass would be difficult to maintain. George Taloumis photo.

Firethorn, *Pyracantha coccinea lalandi.*

Holly, Inkberry, *Ilex glabra.*

Mountain-laurel, *Kalmia latifolia.*

Rhododendron, *Rhododendron maximum, R. catawbiense* and hybrids.

> Note: The evergreen Azaleas, *Rhododendron obtusum* and varieties are hardy only in the South.

DWARF NEEDLE EVERGREENS
(mostly under 5 feet)

Arborvitae, Globe, *Thuja occidentalis globosa* and other dwarf forms.

Juniper, many forms of *Juniperus*, low and spreading, often beautifully colored and textured; silvery or blue-green in summer, purple-bronze in winter. Notably *J. chinensis hetzi, J. horizontalis plumosa, J. pfitzeriana,* and *J. sabina.* Taller forms, upright or rounded, are *J. c. keteleeri, J. c. pyramidalis,* and *J. scopulorum.*

Pine, Mugho, *Pinus mugo,* compact, broad-bushy, dark.

Yew, *Taxus media,* various horticultural forms, and *T. cuspidata nana,* wide-spreading, low.

HEDGES

Shrubs provide the material for hedges, no matter how formal or informal. For low upkeep, choose a slow-growing hedge that will need clipping only once a year, maybe only once every two or three years. It is easy with a fast-growing hedge to become a slave—once a month you give the weekend to trimming your hedge. If you do any hedge pruning, remember to keep the plants wider at the base than at the top. This lets light in to the lowest growth on the hedge—and keeps it lively and full there. Flowering shrubs like forsythia, lilac, or weigela used for hedging should never be clipped into formal shapes.

SHRUBS FOR LOW, CLIPPED HEDGES
(3 feet high or less)

Barberry, *Berberis* species and varieties, especially *B. thunbergi* and its dwarf red variety.

Box, Korean, *Buxus microphylla koreana*, low-growing, slow.

Currant, Alpine, *Ribes alpinus*, dense, very hardy.

Euonymus, *Euonymus fortunei vegetus* and *E. patens*.

Holly, Short-leaved, *Ilex convexa*.

Ninebark, *Physocarpus opulifolius nanus*.

Pachistima, *Pachistima canbyi*, beautiful edging plant, under 1 foot.

Privet, Amur, *Ligustrum amurense*, very hardy and tough.

Privet, Regel's, *Ligustrum obtusifolium regelianum*, graceful, branching.

Viburnum, *Viburnum opulus nanum*, fine for moist, heavy soil.

SHRUBS FOR MEDIUM AND TALL CLIPPED HEDGES
(4 to 8 feet high)

Arborvitae, *Arborvitae occidentalis*, evergreen.

Buckthorn, *Rhamnus cathartica*, withstands drought.

Hemlock, *Tsuga canadensis*, evergreen.

Juniper, *Juniperus chinensis keteleeri*, evergreen.

Rock-spray, *Cotoneaster acutifolia* and *C. divaricata*.

Spruce, Colorado, *Picea pungens*, blue-green, evergreen.

Yew, *Taxus media hicksi* and *T. m. hatfieldi*, the latter more spreading. Evergreen.

SHRUBS FOR UNCLIPPED HEDGES

Almost any shrub, deciduous or evergreen, can be used in quantity, unclipped, to make an effective and sizable hedge. But sooner or later some judicious pruning will be needed to keep it from becoming an overgrown and overwhelming boundary, out of proportion, in all likelihood, to the rest of the garden. Dead

Needle evergreens and opuntia cactus give foliage color in all seasons for this near-desert garden, deeply mulched with crushed stone to eliminate weeding and conserve soil moisture.

wood and *old* wood should be removed on forsythia, hibiscus, lilacs, mock-orange, viburnums, and others. Suckers at the base will have to be kept down. Privet, allowed to grow naturally, can make a fine background in time but tends to become top heavy. And some flowering shrubs—mock-orange for one—may at times need entirely too much spraying against black aphids. Shrubs which do not grow too high are the most manageable, and when in bloom show themselves off at eye-level. Here are some of the best low-maintenance ones:

Beauty-bush, *Kolkwitzia amabilis,* to 7 ft. Arching branches almost to the ground, pink flowers in late spring.

Burning-bush, *Euonymus alatus,* to 5 ft. Blazing autumn color. Also a dwarf form.

Flowering Quince, *Chaenomeles* hybrids (often sold as *Cydonia*), to 6 ft. or kept down to 3 or 4 ft. Early spring bloom, white, pink, or red. Very hardy.

Forsythia, *Forsythia* 'Lynwood Gold', to 6 ft.

Honeysuckle, *Lonicera tatarica,* 6 ft. Rose-pink flowers in spring. Charming small leaves.

Lilac, *Syringa sweginflexa,* to 5 ft. Tidy habit, long trusses of pink flowers in late May. Also selected named hybrids of other lilac species (consult your nurseryman).

Rose, *Polyantha,* 1 to 1½ ft., blooming all summer.

Rose, *Rosa rugosa,* excellent foliage, thorny barrier, "wild-rose" flowers all summer, autumn fruits.

Sweet Pepper-bush, *Clethra alnifolia,* to 5 ft. Spikes of fragrant white flowers in August, good foliage. Also a pink variety, *rosea,* lower-growing. Both good in moist soil.

Viburnum, *Viburnum opulus nanum,* to 2 ft. Dense, vigorous, very hardy. Flowers inconspicuous. Will thrive in heavy moist soil.

Weigela modern hybrids, 5 to 6 ft. Var. 'Majestueux' 3 to 4 ft. White, pink, or red flowers in late May and June.

CHAPTER VII

FLOWERS:

NOT TOO MANY

Grow the flowers you and your family like best and put the rest of your land in grass, ground-cover, paving, or under a deep mulch. Gather your flower forces in one mass. Concentrate effort. Save time in areas not important to you. Spend it where returns are highest. Work with a plan. In flower beds, keep the combinations simple. Try to achieve the results you want with just a few different flowers, and by making only one major planting in the spring (annuals) and sometimes one in autumn (hardy bulbs that will bloom in spring).

EASY WAYS WITH ANNUALS

Pick up started annual plants in spring at your local garden center on a day that is convenient for setting them out. All you have to do to keep annuals prospering and blooming is to cut off spent blooms before seeds ripen. Biologically all an annual wants to do is to flower, ripen seeds, then die. As long as you keep seeds from ripening, the plant keeps producing blooms in its natural urge to reproduce.

Before you go away on a summer trip, shear back annuals sufficiently to remove most of the current bloom. When you return in a week or two, the plants will be coming into new bloom—much nicer than coming home to a lot of seedy looking plants.

One way to use annuals with great style is to mass a single kind—a bed of Zenith zinnias, for example. Or mass in a monochromatic color scheme. You might put in a bed of 'Pink Cascade' petunia, combined with 'Cherry Sundae' giant hybrid zinnia, 'Pink Heather' sweet alyssum, and other pink-flowered varieties of annuals such as baby's-breath, larkspur, snapdragon, stock, China aster, verbena, phlox, and Sensation cosmos.

Another pleasing way with annual flowers is to develop a scheme providing one strong main color, maybe it will be yellow (marigolds, Gloriosa daisies [rudbeckia], and zinnias), a secondary complementary color, probably blue-to-lavender (ageratum and larkspur), and a dash of a third strong color for sharp accent—maybe it will be scarlet (salvia).

In a shrubbery border there are always places to make pockets of annuals—most kinds grow in the sun. In shade you can use torenia, browallia, impatiens, and semperflorens or wax begonias. Just prepare the soil 8 inches deep. If it is sticky clay or otherwise hard and not easy to dig, add a bale of sphagnum peatmoss to every 200 square feet. Plant, water, and mulch. That is all you have to do for all-season flowers.

If there is a patch of ground even 10 x 10 feet to spare, put in a little-upkeep cutting garden—row on row of annuals from seed packets or from young plants sold at nurseries or wayside stands. Maybe some corms of miniature gladiolus (these are better for cutting than the giant kinds that are mostly stalk). Mulch deeply early in the season. Little or no weeding or watering will then be needed. Sounds too good to be true, but all you do, excepting initial planting, mulching, and mixing 5-10-5 fertilizer into the top inch or two of soil, is to keep the flowers cut, having bouquets all over the house and plenty to spare for friends. You can even put down a systemic fertilizer/pesticide early in the season before planting that will inhibit weed growth and kill sucking insects. Select annual flowers for a cutting garden in colors suited to the interior scheme of your home. All shades and hues are available. Here are favorite kinds for cutting:

Ageratum	Dahlia	Snapdragon
Baby's-breath	Larkspur	Stock
Calendula	Marigold	Verbena
Cornflower	Petunia	Zinnia
Cosmos	Salvia	

Concentrate flowers for maximum impact. Here, cinerarias in a raised planting bed give spring color. If cinerarias aren't available in your area, fill planting bed in autumn with bulbs of tulips, daffodils, and hyacinths for spring bloom. Follow in summer with easy annuals such as petunias, geraniums, or dwarf zinnias. *National Concrete Masonry Association photo.*

85

Left: **Hybrid petunias, especially kinds like the White Cascade variety shown** **are about the quickest and best thing going for summer color in pots, boxes** **tubs, baskets, and planting beds.** *Pan-American Seed Company photo. Right* **For flowers in the shade, plant hybrid impatiens. Colors range from hot orange** **and pinks, through all the pastels, to purest white.** *George W. Park Seed Com-* *pany photo.*

COLOR WITHOUT PAIN.   In a shrubbery or herbaceous perennial border, where the soil has been worked into a friable condition, broadcast seeds of Iceland poppies, California poppies, larkspur, and bachelor's-buttons on Christmas, New Year's, or any other winter day—preferably when there is snow on the ground. These seeds of hardy annuals will nestle into the soil to germinate in the first warm days of spring. The young plants develop with vigor through cool nights and warm days, and produce blooms at the very beginning of the annual-flower season—actually by the time spring bulbs are finishing. When the earliest finish, the hot-summer annuals like petunias and zinnias will be coming into bloom. This idea works best when seeds are sown over cultivated soil; obviously, fewer seeds will survive if they are sown in an area of unprepared soil, for example, an open meadow.

CONTAINER GARDENING.   Pots, tubs, planters, and baskets of movable color can be enjoyed all spring, summer, and fall around the garden—wherever you want flowers for a zing effect—up close or as a focal point for vista. By the terrace or other outdoor living area. By the pool. At the entry. All you have to do for container-grown plants is keep the soil moist, and feed biweekly. There is no stooping to weed, only an occasional minute to trim off spent blooms. This way a few flowering plants give you maximum effect for the least amount of trouble. Put them exactly where you want color at any given moment.

Groupings of container plants are more easily cared for, and make a greater show than single pots or tubs scattered around.

Modular wooden boxes may be grouped or used separately for plantings. Larger planters are more difficult to move than smaller ones, but hold moisture for longer periods of time and make possible a wider selection of plant materials. *American Plywood Association photo.*

Ideas conveyed in a Colonial Williamsburg garden: A circle of grass under a wide-spreading tree, with a narrow flower border around the edge. Frame the area with boxwood or yew (occasional clipping needed). Make only two plantings each year: Tulip (or daffodil) bulbs in autumn for spring flowers, and started annuals, such as petunias, in late spring for abundant color all summer. *Colonial Williamsburg photo.*

Easy-to-keep-tidy service entrance, *above*, features brick surfaces and slightly raised planting beds. Daffodils bloom through English ivy ground-cover, in shade of flowering dogwood. For seasonal color: Pots of tulips at doorstep, purple wisteria on wall, red azaleas in background. William L. Koenig, L.A.

Making the most of an entrance from a city street, *above*: bricks, stones, and evergreens (pine, yew, and English ivy). Robert Fenton, L.A.

Flowering dogwood and redbud trees, *below*, with azaleas underneath, give a wave of spring bloom. White birch and evergreen trees provide winter interest.

Terrace with azaleas and rhododendrons for spring color, *left*, has *Vinca minor* ground-cover. After flowers, the evergreen foliage makes a pleasing background all summer. *George Taloumis photo.*

Violas in a handsome terra-cotta strawberry barrel thrive in cool spring weather; then you replace with dwarf marigolds (in sun) or dwarf impatiens (in shade) for nonstop bloom until autumn frost. *Chevron Chemical Company photo.*

Container plants give flowers where and when you want them. In partial shade, a red-and-white fuchsia blooms. Toward the sun, there are pots of fancyleaf geraniums, purple lobelia, and lavender-blue browallia. *George Taloumis photo.*

Casual but neat plantings provide a smooth transition from brick patio to woodland through use of railroad-tie risers, pebble mulch, creeping junipers, and English ivy groundcover. Landscaping by Goldberg and Rodler.

A narrow side yard organized for easy care has an unclipped hedge for privacy, English ivy to carpet the ground, and brick walkway. *George Taloumis photo.*

Pleasant formality at the street, without weekly maintenance, is achieved by islands of English ivy between paths of brick. Ivy also covers ground under hemlock hedge. Landscaping by Goldberg and Rodler.

Only snow changes the appearance of this Japanese-influenced garden, with no-upkeep gravel, evergreens underplanted with pachysandra, a small shade tree, and stone sculpture. *George Taloumis photo.*

Designed for living, the property, *above*, makes the most of outdoor space while keeping maintenance at a minimum. Tubs of geraniums and ivy give color without work. The shrub beds are mulched with wood chips, the planting pockets for trees filled with vinca. The broad sweep of lawn is easy to mow and perfect for croquet. *Ezra Stoller Associates photo.*

Sand pinks (*Armeria maritima*) bloom in planting pocket, *left*, arranged in the modular concept of the patio. Pebble mulch keeps out weeds, saves soil moisture.

Also, try repetition of the same plant in the same size pot. This modular look is appropriate with contemporary architecture; for example, nine 10-inch clay tubs of dwarf French marigolds, all of the same color, spaced out evenly in rows, three by three.

CONTAINER PLANTS
(except where noted, buy well-started plants)

FOR SUN	FOR SHADE	FOR HOT, DRY SITE
African Daisy	Achimenes	Crassula
Ageratum	*Begonia semper-*	Kalanchoe
Begonia semperflorens	*florens*	Portulaca (seed or
Geranium	Caladium (tubers)	plants)
Marigold (seed or plants)	Coleus	Sedum
Nicotiana 'White Bedder'	Impatiens	Sempervivum
Petunia		
Salvia		
Verbena		
Zinnia 'Thumbelina'		
(seed)		

SPRING-FLOWERING BULBS. Some kinds of hardy, spring-flowering bulbs need almost no care after the first planting. Drift daffodils, scillas, crocus, snowdrops, aconites, and species tulips. These can go into meadow areas where they come up and bloom while the grass is short in spring. By the time the grass grows up, or just a little later, even if it is to be mowed, the bulb foliage will have matured so that clipping is not harmful. These are fine, in any rustic setting, but also near the house there is always room to bunch daffodils and other spring bulbs. Only the show-size hybrid tulips, the Darwin and breeder types, and Dutch hyacinths seem to require formal plantings, but even these can be placed in small or large groupings wherever you want spring flowers. Plant in sun or under deciduous trees, whose leaves will not be then developed enough to give too much shade. Ideally, bulbs need deeply prepared, well-drained soil, but in fact they will endure far from perfect conditions, returning spring after spring with the most welcome flowers of the season—those that come first.

PERENNIAL FLOWERS. The best of these stay on and on, multiplying and giving a better show each succeeding year. Some are attractive in foliage as well as in flower. Division and replanting is in order about every third or fourth year, excepting gas-plant and peony—which can be left for decades. Some others do well for a year or two, then decline or disappear entirely—pyrethrum and stokesia, for example—so omit these. Perennials sprout up from the ground in spring, freeze to the ground in fall, come back the next spring.

Perennials may be used in countless low-upkeep ways. Plant in bays with shrubbery as a backdrop; in a bed by the terrace; in a formal garden; in a cutting garden. Use them alone, or in combination with spring-flowering bulbs to begin the season, and with low shrubs, small trees, and annuals. Most perennials need sun. A few—daylilies, hosta, and monarda—can take shade provided the soil is well prepared, humusy, and moist. Astilbe and almost all ferns need shade.

Start perennials by obtaining clumps from a local nursery or by mail—in spring (preferably) or in early fall. Some are easy and inexpensive to start from seeds—Shasta daisies, pinks, and cerastium, for example. Blackberry-lily (belamcanda) even blooms the first year from seeds sown in March.

The aim of most of us in planting a perennial border is to have a flower bed attractive to view from the house with enough flowers for bouquets. It doesn't take many different kinds of perennials to achieve this goal. You can do it with a selection of peonies, followed by daylilies that bloom from mid-spring to late summer, and potted chrysanthemums bought in bud for fall display. Daylilies (hemerocallis) are the most notable for a long flowering season with almost no maintenance. There are hundreds of varieties, but this baker's dozen will give May-to-September bloom.

DAYLILIES FOR FIVE MONTHS OF BLOOM
(An early-to-late sequence of varieties)

Queen of Gonzales	Frances Fay	Postscript
Golden Chimes	Orange Monarch	Merry Sun
Fairy Wings	Mission Moonlight	Carved Gold
Grecian Gift	Late and Lovely	Last Dance
	George Cunningham	

Left: The surest and easiest way to have early spring flowers is to plant bulbs of tulips, hyacinths, and daffodils in the fall. Formal bedding designs require annual replanting with fresh bulbs, but when naturalized in a semi-wild area, or planted in a mixed perennial border, the same bulbs can be left in the ground year after year for flowers every spring without any maintenance work. The leaves must then not be removed until yellow (the leaves feed the bulbs), but before then you can interplant started annuals. *Netherlands Flower-bulb Institute photo. Right:* Floribundas require the least upkeep of all roses and give an almost constant display of flowers from early summer until fall frost. Periodic spraying with an all-purpose rose spray keeps them healthy. Maintenance in this garden is further reduced by edging the bed with redwood and covering the ground with stone chips. *American Association of Nurserymen photo.*

91

Left: Old herbs cultivated in a contemporary style: Basil planted in clay pots will need occasional clipping, and provide seasoning for the kitchen. An interesting and handsome edging for a rose bed. *Right:* Mint takes a new turn, trained on a circular wire frame. A high-maintenance whimsy like this is one way to spend some of the time you save from low-upkeep landscaping. Besides, mint smells good, and is pleasant to clip for flavoring. *Chevron Chemical Company photos.*

Planning a perennial border that is rich in different kinds of flowers and arranging each so that the plants are complementary, with areas of the border coming pleasantly in and out of bloom, is a lot of fun, but in the same complicated way as duplicate bridge. There are astronomical variables. Sketch the size garden you want to scale on a sheet of paper—graph paper is fine, or draw, using ¼ inch to equal 1 foot. Study catalog descriptions, and indicate your choices on the plan. Usually a minimum of three each should be put in a clump but one peony or one dictamnus makes a pleasant accent. You can plan a border mostly for spring flowers with a few in summer and fall; flowers from spring to frost; or a border in partial to full shade—featuring ferns, hostas, daylilies, and nearly wild flowers such as epimedium, violets, and primroses.

EASY PERENNIALS FOR EDGING AND CARPETING

Alyssum 'Basket of Gold'	Chives	Primrose
Artemisia 'Silver Mound'	Chrysanthemum,	Santolina, Cushion
Aster, dwarf hardy	dwarf	*Sedum spurium*
Bellflower, Carpathian	Coral Bells	Snow-in-summer
Bellflower, Serbian	Iris, dwarf bearded	(Cerastium)
Candytuft, hardy	Nepeta	Violets (white)
	Pinks (Dianthus)	Woolly Yarrow
	Plumbago	

MEDIUM-HEIGHT PERENNIALS
(for midway from the front to the back of the border)

Astilbe (shade)	Chrysanthemum	Monarda
Baby's-breath	Columbine	Peony
Balloonflower	Coreopsis	Oriental Poppy
Bleeding Heart	Daylily	Peony
Butterfly Weed	Feverfew	Shasta Daisy
	Gas-plant	Veronica

TALL PERENNIALS

(for the back of the border or garden; for making large-scale flower arrangements, especially in containers to stand on the floor)

Achillea 'Gold Plate'	Globe-thistle	Lily
Anchusa	Goldenglow	Lupine
Artemisia 'Silver King'	Helenium	Lythrum
Daylily	Hollyhock	*Phlox paniculata*
Foxglove	Iris, tall bearded, Japanese, Sibc-rian, Spuria	Rose-mallow
		Sunflower
		Tritoma

PERENNIALS FOR A HOT, DRY SITE

Baby's-breath	Gaillardia	Sea-holly
Balloonflower	Globe-thistle	(Eryngium)
Butterfly Weed	Gloriosa Daisy	Sea-pink (Armeria)
Coreopsis	Golden Marguerite	*Sedum spectabile*
Daylily	Iris, bearded	Sunflower, perennial
	Pinks	Yarrow (Achillea)

ROSES FOR CUTTING. The cry of many writers on low-maintenance gardening is apt to be: "No roses!" We do not agree. The modern hybrid roses—grandifloras, floribundas, and many hybrid teas—require no more than planting properly in a reasonably well-prepared hole in the spring. By June there will be bloom. And no matter how no-maintenance you want your garden, someone around the house will want flowers to cut. The floribundas give bouquets of bloom on every stem. Hybrid teas give long-stemmed individual flowers. All modern varieties bloom off and on from May or June until frost.

Our maintenance program for a dozen rosebushes is more pleasure than pain. Cut the blooms, either as they open for arrangements indoors, or when they are spent. Water when dry. Feed about three times a year: early spring, late spring, and late summer. Once every ten days to two weeks apply an all-purpose aerosol rose spray to control pest and disease. There is no mess or fuss in this easy, quick, and convenient control. As growth begins in the spring remove all dead stems, and cut back the live canes to about 12 inches. Neither of us goes to the trouble of hilling up the bushes for winter protection. Either they make it through the winter without bother, or they don't. We find in a bed of a dozen roses that about three will be lost in an average winter. These are removed in the spring and replaced, usually with new varieties of special interest.

HERBS, PLEASANT AND PRACTICAL.   Herbs smell good. They are fun to have handy by the kitchen for seasoning. Some of them are pretty in the garden. As a group, they tend to grow unruly. The way to handle them easily, so they make a decent appearance, is to plant in large pots, or to grow them in restricted areas where bricks or redwood frames define beds and give organization to the garden. Then the herbs can be neatly trimmed back when necessary with a minimum of trouble. Chives are beautiful in bloom. Lavender is sensational. Then you will want basil, peppermint, sage, summer savory, dill, parsley, and thyme. The size and numbers of herbs will depend on whether you like the idea of having them around to look at and smell, or really plan to use them in the kitchen.

Make room in your herb garden for some salad vegetables in the spring—three kinds of lettuce, scallions, and radishes. Of course you will want some staked hybrid tomatoes. You can espalier them, but this gets to be high upkeep. Grow some cherry tomatoes in pots, tubs, or boxes. They are decorative this way, and the crop is easy to harvest.

CHAPTER VIII

ᛌᚱᛌᚱᛌᚱᛌᚱᛌᚱᛌᚱᛌᚱᛌᚱᛌ

YOUR LAWN—

WHAT HAVE YOU?

ᛌᚱᛌᚱᛌᚱᛌᚱᛌᚱᛌᚱᛌᚱᛌᚱ   With the purchase of an older house, even the wary buyer can inherit a lawn that is a disaster. A basically healthy lawn can also turn into an eyesore without the right care.

If you cringe when you glance at your front lawn and feel in danger of being labeled a slum landlord, the time for renovation or installation of a completely new lawn is at hand.

Whether to renovate or not can be a complicated decision. On the one hand, if you planted and nurtured the lawn yourself you may feel paternal toward it. Since the lawn seems to have betrayed the hand that fed, cut, and trimmed it, you may want to bury that ungrateful sod. Try not to let your feelings get in the way of the facts. If at all possible, save the lawn.

There are times, however, when it is absolutely necessary to plow the lawn under. If it is improperly drained because of the nature of the soil itself, or if more than 50 per cent of the area is bare or host to weeds and undesirable grasses, you will have to tear it up with a plow, tiller, or spade, apply a soil sterilant, and turn directly to Chapter 9 for instructions on establishing a new lawn.

RENOVATION

The time to renovate cool-season grasses (bluegrass, for example) is early fall or spring. Preferably early fall, when the ground is still warm enough for germination and when weeds are less of a threat. Spring is the time to work with warm-season grasses (Bermuda, for example).

First step is to cut the grass to its optimum height: about 1½ inches for cool-season grasses, 1 inch for warm-season grasses.

96

This may require several mowings since not more than a quarter of the leaf surface should be removed at any one time. Space the mowings several days apart. Catch the clippings while mowing if you can. Then give the lawn a vigorous going over with a bamboo or steel rake to remove dead grass and other debris.

If the lawn has been used for play, the soil may be compacted so that air, water and fertilizer cannot penetrate. To test for compaction, push a pencil deep into the ground in various parts of the lawn. If it goes in easily, you can consider the soil porous enough. If you really have to force it, aeration is in order.

Rent an aerator from a local equipment dealer, nurseryman, or landscape gardener. If possible, get the type that lifts plugs out of the soil rather than one that merely punches holes. The plugs have to be picked up, but the operation is far more effective.

Having done this, you now have a lawn full of small holes, with sparse grass and large quantities of weeds, but you are making headway.

Apply chemicals to control weeds, insects, and grass diseases that you have determined are present in the lawn. In order to intelligently treat your lawn, you must be able to diagnose the ailments. You don't need to know the name of every weed, but you do need to know the basic types, as well as the symptoms of insect and disease attack. You can learn a lot just by reading the labels at your garden-supply store. Chances are good that you will find the pesticide industry's latest products, and in formulations suited to your region. Follow package instructions to the letter.

BROADLEAF AND GRASSY WEEDS

The initial forays into horticulture can be a nightmare for the novice. The use of complicated botanical names in Latin and several common names for the same plant seems to be a conspiracy to keep gardening only for professionals. Understanding of weeds is no less confusing. On the surface everything seems clear enough. There are two types of weeds—broadleaf and grassy.

Unfortunately, one man's grass may be another's grassy weed, and so-called broadleaf weeds frequently have extremely small and narrow leaves. As a guide, remember that a grassy weed always resembles grass.

APPLYING CHEMICAL CONTROLS

Chemical weed control is the greatest labor-saver in lawn care. Fifteen minutes with the right chemical will do a better job than hours of hand labor. Most broadleaf weeds can be knocked out with 2,4-D or MCPP. Control annual weeds such as crabgrass by applying a pre-emergence killer in early spring at about the time you see forsythia blooming in your neighborhood. Persistent perennial weed grasses *may* have to be hand-pulled.

Use a mechanical spreader to apply dry chemicals over the lawn. If you are treating a large area with liquid chemicals, rent or buy a tank pressure sprayer. A hose-end attachment is good for smaller areas. For very small lawns, an aerosol spray will serve the purpose.

When spraying, hold the nozzle close to the weeds, and keep spraying until they are really wet. Don't expect weeds to wilt and die before your eyes; results are not immediately apparent.

If one application does not work, follow up with the same chemical in two weeks. Apply these herbicides according to instructions on the container. Do not overdose; this adds to the cost and may damage desirable plants.

HERBICIDES

The herbicides (weed-killers) recommended, such as 2,4-D and MCPP, are available under various trade names. Since they kill by speeding up the growth process so that broadleaf weeds actually grow themselves to death, they are not selective. Use them with care or they will damage ornamental plants growing nearby. Spray on windless days; even then shield desirable plants, and hold the nozzle close to the weeds. Weed-killers are most effective when temperatures are above 65 degrees. Apply when rain is not expected for at least twenty-four hours. Do not use weed-killers on lawns that are less than six months old. Although they are safe for well-established turf, they can injure young grass seedlings and newly laid sod.

SOIL STERILANTS

If weeds are spreading and nothing seems to work, there are several chemicals that simply sterilize the area and quickly dissipate, leaving the soil clean and ready for reseeding.

Vapam, Mylone, and calcium cyanamide are the three sterilants that are safe for homeowner use.

Beware of using soil sterilants under trees or shrubs since they may affect roots. Since soil sterilants require tilling the soil and careful treatment, restrict their use to an old lawn full of noxious weeds too thoroughly established to pull or kill with selective chemicals.

CRABGRASS

The homeowner's Weed Enemy Number One is crabgrass. It is the most difficult to control since each plant produces thousands of seeds. Crabgrass doesn't come up all at once, but sprouts through a prolonged hot summer, when conditions are conducive to its germination.

As crabgrass emerges it resembles a fat spear, apple-green in color. The weed's flat stems spread out fast. Lying low, they are difficult to cut. The weed is hard to destroy after it has gotten started because chemicals have to be sprayed frequently for full control. If you had crabgrass last year, the most effective method of removal is to apply a pre-emergence crabgrass killer in early spring, say March. If you let spring pass, live with the crabgrass until fall. Through summer, cut the grass high (leave it relatively tall), since the best crabgrass deterrent lies in encouraging lawn grass to grow higher and denser than the weed.

The most efficient weed-killers for fall application are pre-emergence compounds containing calcium arsenate and DSMA. Apply as directed on the package. A follow-up application the following spring will increase effectiveness.

UNPLEASANT INSECTS

Contemporary homeowners, more accustomed to digging into onion dip than soil, are usually horrified to find that the well-fertilized earth under their lawn is host to a multitude of creepy crawlies. Insect pests can do extensive damage both above and below ground if they are not recognized and stopped early. The first step in control is identification.

GRUBS, which are the larvae of beetles, do extensive damage to grass by feeding on the roots. Japanese beetles, chafers, May beetles, and Asiatic beetles are among the most frequent trouble-makers. Most adults lay eggs underground in late summer, and the larvae hatch and begin feeding on the grass roots. When cold weather arrives, the larvae move deeper underground and return near the surface in spring. The adult then emerges in late May or June.

Grub-damaged lawns fade quickly and die out in hot weather. Sections can be lifted like a carpet after grubs have gnawed away the roots. Apply chlordane, dieldrin, or heptachlor in early fall or spring after thaw. Applications are effective for years. After applying, water the lawn to rinse chemicals into the soil. Milky disease spore dust may also be used to grub-proof the lawn, but this biological control may be tricky to use, and it can take several years to establish itself in the lawn.

CHINCH BUGS, which are small and red-colored when nymphs and black as adults, attack bentgrass and fescues. These tiny insects are only $\frac{1}{5}$ inch long when mature. *Damage usually shows up in humid midsummer. Areas of grass turn brown in ever widening patches.* Chinch bugs are easily detected by pushing a bottomless tin can into the grass along the edge of the damaged areas and filling it with water. If present, they will float to the surface.

Diazinon is an effective control and should be applied only after the ground has been thoroughly watered. Sevin is an alternative. Several applications during the summer may be needed.

SOD WEBWORMS are sophisticated little creatures. They come out only at night. During the day they loll in silk-lined tubes close to the surface. They prefer dining indoors and chew off grass to haul back to their burrows for meals at home. *If sod webworms are present, the moths that lay the eggs will fly around your feet as you walk across infested turf.* Before turning into caterpillars, the larva is light brown and about ¾ inch long. Treat with heptachlor, aldrin, chlordane, or dieldrin.

CUTWORMS are smooth, nearly naked caterpillars. Similar to sod webworms, only twice the size, they vary from 1 to 2 inches when fully grown. They are marked with dull and indistinct spots and longitudinal stripes. Control with granular formulations of chlordane, dieldrin, or heptachlor.

LAWN DISEASES

Sometimes a lawn will just wilt and begin to die for no apparent reason. The slightly desperate homeowner sprays, fertilizes, waters, and still the grass wanes. If nothing seems to help, chances are your sickly lawn has some fungus disease. Sound vague? Well, unfortunately, it is difficult even for experts to identify a fungus disease. There are classic symptoms, but lawn diseases rarely exhibit the symptoms clearly enough for the novice to recognize.

If you suspect a fungus disease, apply a control. There are all-purpose types available at garden-supply stores. It will do no good to till the area and reseed since the spores will remain. If portions of your lawn are repeatedly attacked by fungus, don't fight it. Sometimes soil and moisture conditions encourage fungus. Remove the maintenance trap and plant a ground-cover like English ivy, pachysandra, or vinca.

BARE SPOTS

Dig up bare spots about 6 inches deep in order to uncover any debris that may be present. Then spread fertilizer uniformly over the area. If the area will get foot traffic, work in compost or peat-moss.

If your grass is grown from seed, sprinkle it evenly over the area on a calm day—about thirty-five to forty seeds per square inch of surface. Sow the same type of lawn grass mixture as the rest of the lawn unless the area is very shady. Tamp the seeds firmly into the soil with a hoe or the back of a flat spade. Don't cover the seed; leave it exposed to the sunlight to insure maximum germination. Keep the soil moist by watering daily, but not flooding, until the first blades of grass appear. Frequent sprinkling not only helps the seed take root but also keeps it from blowing away. Much sprinkling can be avoided by covering seeded areas with polyethylene sheets secured by stones. Evaporation is reduced and seeds germinate quickly. Remove the covering at first sign of growth, and water again.

AREAS OF HEAVY SHADE

Heavy shade can make life difficult for most grasses. It is the area under trees that is most frequently bare of grass. The tree takes most of the moisture and nutrients from the grass while restricting sunlight enough to lessen its food-making ability. Planting ground-covers under shade trees is a good, low-upkeep practice, but if you must have grass, here's how:

Apply enough fertilizer for both the tree and the grass and water enough to keep at least the top 6 inches of soil moistened during the grass-growing season. Also cut the grass quite tall, 2 to 3 inches high, permitting extra green leaf to compensate for the somewhat restricted sunlight. Prune away the lower limbs of the trees where this does not interfere with their natural shape and good looks. Watering under the trees should be much more prolonged than in open areas, and fertilizer should be applied twice as often as on the rest of the lawn.

Plant creeping red fescue or other shade-loving grass that will match the color and texture of the remainder of the lawn. In the northern part of the United States, the best shade grasses are red fescue, Chewings fescue, and rough bluegrass—in that order. St. Augustine, zoysia, and centipede are the best shade grasses in the South.

Once your lawn has been reestablished, set up a program for maintenance (see Chapter 9). For low-upkeep lawns, keep basically healthy grass in good condition instead of letting it run down periodically and going through massive renovation. A healthy lawn will actually prevent invasion by weeds, pests, and fungus, and thus minimize work.

CHAPTER IX

A LAWN

IS WHAT YOU MAKE IT

555555555555555555 If you want the best lawn on the block—forget the low-upkeep concept. A perfectly manicured lawn requires a yard slave—either you hire one or become one. However, you can have a *decent* lawn with minimum maintenance requirements if you choose the right grass, prepare the soil properly, and keep the lawn basically healthy.

Choosing the right grass is important to success in building a new lawn because each species has certain requirements of temperature, light, water, nutrients, and other growth essentials that make it more suitable for one area than another.

LET'S TAKE THE MYSTERY OUT OF BUYING LAWN GRASSES

Lawn grasses are grouped into cool-season and warm-season types. Cool-season grasses make their maximum growth during the cool months of the year. Although they remain green in the summer, they are semi-dormant then and exhibit only limited growth during this time. Warm-season grasses are those that make their maximum growth in warm months. Most of these grasses do not survive winter in northern areas. With few exceptions, they turn brown with the first frost and remain dormant or at least semi-dormant until spring.

The map on page 104 shows the sections of the country where cool- and warm-season grasses grow best.

Your local nurseryman will probably carry only grasses or mixtures that are adapted to your region. Let's take a look at the most desirable cool- and warm-season grasses, with an eye to their maintenance needs.

COOL-SEASON GRASSES

Most cool-season grasses sold today come in a mixture. This may be confusing to you, but the mixtures have been prepared with purpose. Conditions vary from one area of your lawn to another, and in each area, the species that succeeds best will take over; in addition, some of the grasses in each mixture are more susceptible to certain diseases than others, and when a susceptible species succumbs to a disease, one of the more resistant strains will take over.

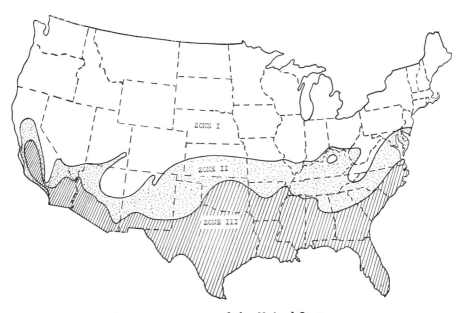

Lawn grass zones of the United States

ZONE I.   Area of cool-season grasses such as blue-grass.

ZONE II.   Both cool-season and warm-season grasses will survive here, but they require special care.

ZONE III.   Area of warm-season grasses.

When you are buying grass seed, it is definitely not the time to economize. As a matter of fact, beware of cut-rate seeds. For example, high-quality Merion Kentucky bluegrass is quite expensive, but there are inexpensive Merion Mixtures on the market. However, these will occasionally contain as little as 1 percent actual Merion. This doesn't mean that you should buy according to price or even name brand. Check the label for the mixture inside. The label on a box of lawn seed is most important. By law it contains the actual amount of all seed contained in the package.

Avoid mixtures containing large amounts of annual ryegrass. It sprouts quickly, but, as the name implies, it does not generally survive into the second year. Should some plants last in favored locations, they become coarse and clumpy. However, a *small* percentage of ryegrass is useful when covering a newly seeded slope, since it will give quick cover for protection while perennial grasses get established.

Forget mixtures with even a small amount of coarse grass, unless you are sowing them in an old field that is already full of weeds. If you want an attractive lawn, you really must sow only fine-textured grasses.

KENTUCKY BLUEGRASS is the basic grass for northern areas of this country. It is a hardy, long-lived, thick turf-forming grass of medium texture. Prominent selected varieties are Fylking, Kenblue, Merion, Newport, Park, and Windsor. Merion and Windsor are two of the most popular varieties. Both have good tolerance to close mowing and hot weather. However, they require a high level of fertility, and Merion is subject to leaf rust.

RED FESCUE, next to Kentucky Blue, is the most popular cool-season lawn grass. It is excellent for shade and will survive with little water and fertilizer. Familiar varieties include Chewings, Highlight, Pennlawn, Ranier, and Ruby. Fescue is slow-growing, but it will resist considerable wear.

A mixture of 70 percent creeping red fescue and 30 percent bluegrass makes an excellent minimum-maintenance lawn of cool-season grasses.

BENTGRASS, of all the cool-season types, makes the most beautiful turf. It forms a dense uniform mat of rich green. But if you yearn for low upkeep, forget it, unless you restrict your lawn to a very small area where you can have that putting-green look. Bentgrass requires frequent mowing, ample feeding, pest control, and occasional thinning. Some suggested varieties include Penncross, Seaside, Astoria, Exeter, Colonial, and Kingstown.

WARM-AREA GRASSES

The textures and looks of warm-area grasses vary greatly, so they are rarely sold in mixtures. It is therefore even more important in Southern regions to choose carefully when selecting the grass for your lawn.

BERMUDA is the number one grass of the South. It grows vigorously and forms a low dense turf that tolerates heat and close mowing. Bermuda may be popular, but it demands regular attention: monthly feeding and twice weekly mowing at low height. Common Bermuda grass cannot endure shade and is the only strain established by seed. The others like U-3 and Tiflawn are propagated vegetatively.

ZOYSIA, once established, is among the finest Southern lawn grasses. It makes a thick cushiony sod that resists most afflictions. It can stand moderate shade, close clipping, and does not require much maintenance. Zoysia is very slow to grow, and even when established does not have to be cut often. Most popular varieties are Meyer and Emerald. They are propagated vegetatively. Zoysia requires less attention than Bermuda.

CENTIPEDE is not the most elegant of grasses but it will result in what can be termed an "adequate" Southern lawn. It actually resents too much attention, and prefers acid soils. Centipede can be established from seed, but most often is vegetatively propagated. It grows well in shade and on poor, sandy soils.

ST. AUGUSTINE is a coarse-textured but not unattractive grass popular in coastal areas from the Carolinas to east Texas. It is tolerant of shade and adapted to mucky soils and warm, moist climates. Sod can be purchased inexpensively. Unfortunately, St. Augustine is susceptible to disease, to invasion by chinch bug and other difficult-to-control maladies. The problems are compounded because it is not tolerant to 2,4-D and arsenate weed-killers.

BAHIA is popular in the deep South because it is relatively care-free, tolerant, and can be started from seed. It thrives in most soils in shade or sun with moderate attention. For low maintenance, Bahia is better than St. Augustine, and for looks it tops centipede. The Argentine variety produces fewer difficult-to-mow seedheads than the more prevalent Pensacola.

CARPETGRASS requires soil with high moisture content all year long. It spreads rapidly and produces dense, compact, coarse-textured turf. It can be established by seeding, sprigging, and laying sod. For Gulf Coast only.

DICHONDRA, widely used in southern California, is a grass substitute for warm-area lawns. It has rounded, heart-shaped leaves on trailing stems. Dichondra is beautiful, requires little mowing, but needs frequent feeding and watering. Start from seed or sprigs, but don't attempt to grow it if temperatures in your area go below freezing.

INSTALLING A NEW LAWN

SOIL PREPARATION. If you want an easy-care lawn, make it healthy at the start and then keep it that way. To borrow an adage, "As the soil is prepared, so grows the grass." Grass derives life from sun and soil. You can't do much about the sun, but you can improve the soil. A properly prepared soilbed will give the lawn the right start because grass roots will spread easily. Later it will reduce the problems and costs of the mature lawn.

First determine the present condition of your soil. There are two methods. You can send soil samples from different parts of the lawn area to your local county agent or state agricultural extension service (check the Yellow Pages). Or you can buy an inexpensive soil testing kit and do it yourself. With either method, the soil samples will tell you the conditioners needed to add to the soil, the acidity level, and how to raise and lower it, and the kind and amount of fertilizer to be added.

Rent a rototiller to loosen the soil so that it can be worked. Don't work soil when it is wet. When tilling, avoid beating the soil into a fluff. Fluffed soil forms a compact mass when wet. Remove stones and debris. The soil must be graded evenly so there are no pockets in which water can collect. The slope should drop gently away from the house for proper drainage. Use a hand rake for leveling and spreading.

Now is the time to make use of the information from your soil testing. Additives may include lime, superphosphate, peatmoss, well-rotted manure, fully decomposed sawdust, sewage sludge, peanut hulls, or rice hulls. Do a thorough job of incorporating additives into the soil. Failure to do so will create layers that may cause future trouble. Then add a complete fertilizer (one containing nitrogen, phosphorus, and potash). Rake it lightly into the soil. Add 25 pounds of a complete fertilizer with a ratio of 20-10-10 or 12-8-6 for each 1,000 square feet of lawn. The numbers on the fertilizer bag identify the percentage of each component in the mixture. All brands use the same order, first nitrogen, then phosphorus, and finally potash.

Once you have added the fertilizer and double-checked to make sure there are no low spots, you are ready to consider the grass.

ESTABLISHING LAWN GRASS.   There are three methods of establishing lawn grass: seeding, sodding, and vegetative planting. The method you use will depend on the type grass you choose and the rapidity of cover desired. Seeding is the cheapest method and does not require much work; sodding gives an instant effect but is comparatively expensive; vegetative planting requires work but is the only way to start some excellent low-maintenance grasses, such as zoysia and centipede.

SOWING SEED.   The best time to sow cool-season grass seed is the fall. Early spring is best for warm-season types. Cool-season types may also be started in early spring. If you are caught without having seeded by the time early summer rolls around and you don't want to spend the hot weather with a dustbowl on your hands, sow a temporary lawn of ryegrass and then in the fall plow it under as fertilizer before planting a permanent grass mixture.

A mechanical spreader is the safest and quickest way to broadcast seed. The seed package gives the correct setting. It will also tell the coverage possible with the seed you have. Divide the seed in half and spread the first half over the entire lawn area using the spreader setting at one-half the recommended opening. Use the second half of the seed by walking crosswise. If you walked north and south the first time, then go east and west the second. Now use the back of your rake or a light roller to bring the seed in contact with the soil.

Mulching with a light covering of weed-free straw or hay will help hold moisture and prevent washing away the seed during watering or rain. Apply evenly and lightly. The grass will grow through the mulch, which will rot and add fertility to the soil.

New seedlings should be kept moist until well established. Once seeds have begun to germinate, they must not dry out or they will die. Light and frequent watering during a seven- to fourteen-day period should be sufficient.

SODDING. Since we don't recommend grass for steep slopes or terraces, the expense of sodding is seldom justified unless complete coverage is needed immediately. To sod, prepare and fertilize the lawn area in the same way as for seeding. Then firm it with a light roller. Sod should not be more than an inch thick. Three-quarter-inch sod will knit to the underlying soil faster than thicker sod. Fit the squares or strips tightly together. After laying the first strip, use a broad board for kneeling to avoid tramping on the prepared seedbed.

Once the sod is laid, tamp it lightly. *Then water regularly.* After it is rooted, topdress with a well-mixed and screened mixture of topsoil, sand, and organic matter. Fill in cracks between sod pieces with a broom or the back of a wooden rake.

VEGETATIVE PLANTING. Seed for warm-season grasses such as zoysia, St. Augustine, centipede, and certain improved Bermudas is not available or does not produce plants that are true to type. These grasses must be planted vegetatively by plugging, strip sodding, or sprigging.

Plugging means planting small plugs or blocks of sod at measured intervals, generally 12 inches apart. They may be set closer together for more rapid coverage. The plugs should be planted tightly in prepared holes and tamped firmly into place.

Strip sodding involves planting strips of sod, 2 to 4 inches wide, end to end in rows 12 inches apart. Firm contact with surrounding soil is necessary.

Sprigging is the planting of individual plants, runners, cuttings, or stolons at spaced intervals. Sprigs or runners are obtained by tearing apart or shredding solid pieces of established sod. The space interval is governed by the spread-rate of the grass, how fast coverage is desired, and the amount of planting material you bought. Lawns may be sprigged at any time during the growing season when adequate moisture is available.

MAINTENANCE PROGRAM FOR LOW UPKEEP

When the snow melts, remove the winter's accumulation of dead grass, leaves, and other debris that can choke off sunlight and water.

Apply a complete fertilizer—one containing nitrogen, phosphorus, and potash—in early spring and fall. Read the instructions carefully and apply evenly so you don't "burn" the lawn. Follow with an extra application of nitrogen in late spring for cool-season grasses. Warm-season grasses will require feedings of nitrogen every four to six weeks through summer. Most lawns, particularly those east of the Mississippi River, should have applications of lime every two or three years.

Apply a pre-emergent crabgrass killer in March or April.

Apply a broadleaf-weed-killer in May or June. Both the fertilizers and weed-killers are a breeze to apply with mechanical spreaders.

Cool-season grasses should be cut at 1¼ to 1½ inches during the spring to thicken the turf so that it can combat crabgrass more effectively. As warm weather sets in, raise the height-of-cut to a range of 1½ to 2½ inches and maintain it at this level for the rest of the growing season. Cut warm-season grasses normally at heights ¾ to 1 inch. Closer cutting during the spring will encourage lateral growth and turf density.

Water during the hot summer months. When needed, water deeply to encourage deep rooting of the grass. Frequent shallow watering draws roots to the surface, weakens the plant, and encourages weeds.

In early fall check for compaction. If it exists, rent an aerator and run it over the lawn.

Set up your maintenance program and then follow it. Healthy grass is easy-care grass.

CHAPTER X

正正正正正正正正正正正正正正

THE AUTOMATED LAWN

正正正正正正正正正正正正正正 On hot summer afternoons, every homeowner dreams of the freedom of totally automated lawn care. Actually, that dream is fast becoming a reality. The development of improved mowing equipment and the widespread use of lawn tractors are a help, but the real liberator of the yard slave is the automatic underground sprinkler system. Probably more overall time is spent hand-watering or moving devices around than any other lawn-care activity. As a result, automatic watering is steadily gaining acceptance. There are over 500,000 home systems in operation today. But there are still many misconceptions about watering in general, and specifically about automatic underground systems.

Are they expensive? Do they use more water? Will installations destroy the present lawn? Should you operate the system at night? Can you install the system yourself? For most homeowners, automation, even the ground-level variety, is clouded in mystery.

Automatic underground sprinkler systems have been around for half a century. However, in recent years the cost has been reduced substantially by new sprinkler heads that give wider coverage, and by the use of plastic pipe. This is more effective and longer lasting than the earlier galvanized, brass, or copper piping.

COST OF AUTOMATIC WATERING

Although the systems still require a major investment for the homeowner, they undoubtedly increase the value of property and can be purchased under a low-cost home-improvement loan. Most systems cost about 10 to 15 cents a square foot. Prices are determined by the system installed, the local cost of labor, the number of trees and shrubs, the shape of your property, and your type of soil.

Part of the investment in a sprinkler system is returned through lower water bills. Most people assume that since an automatic sprinkler system keeps the grass greener and has a set program, it will use more water. But it uses much less than hand-watering since it may be programmed to supply only as much water as is needed for healthy turf. The best-designed systems deliver water only as fast as the soil can absorb it—like a gentle rain—so there is no loss from runoff.

WHEN TO WATER

Automated lawn watering can be scheduled to operate in the early morning—from 4 to 6 a.m.—when water pressure is highest and loss from evaporation and wind is lowest. There is a misconception that watering at night causes fungus to develop. This is only a half-truth. Watering before sunrise washes away dew and actually inhibits fungus and bacteria. A look at the local golf course dispels doubts about night watering. Golf-course superintendents, who are the real pros when it comes to grass, always set their systems to run before sunrise. Daytime watering is limited to cooling the grass during prolonged hot weather.

Lawns are not crisscrossed with trenches and covered with mounds of earth when an underground system is installed. Actually, new pipe-pulling and sodding equipment barely disturbs the lawn. The pulling equipment, which is best for sandy or rock-free soil, has a bar with a pipe attached at the bottom. As the bar moves through the soil, laying the pipe, it leaves only a fine surface slit. In rocky soil, a sodding machine cuts a narrow strip of grass. This is then removed and a machine that digs a trench— 1 to 3 inches wide—is opened to receive the pipe. Once this is laid and the soil and sod replaced, all that shows are two pencil-thin lines. In 7 to 10 days, no evidence of either installation method is visible.

Most important, the average installation can be completed by a professional in one day.

HOW TO INSTALL

The do-it-yourself installation of an underground sprinkler system is a tricky business, and most manufacturers recommend that the work be done by a professional. True, the installation of a simple system can be a pleasant project for the ambitious and less expensive, of course, but don't attempt an installation without a qualified equipment dealer to advise you. This is the way to proceed.

1. Draw a scale plan of the area to be covered. You can use your landscaping plan as a basis. Make sure the locations of outside faucets are indicated.

When drawing a plan for an automatic underground sprinkler system, indicate position of outside faucets. Here two faucets have been used to reduce digging on a small property.

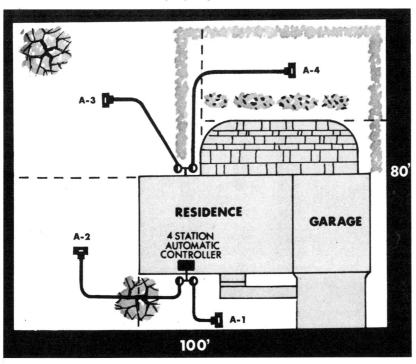

If you may want to water more than just your lawn, shrubs and other plantings can be included in a well-designed system. Special sprinkler heads are available for this purpose. There are also new dual controllers on the market that have two separate watering schedules, so that flower-bed watering can also be automated.

2. Position sprinkler heads on the diagram. To do this properly, you need information on your water supply and pressure. High-flow pressure means maximum-area coverage, low pressure means smaller coverage, and so more heads to cover a given area.

The simplest approach is to call your water department and ask about the water pressure and gallons per minute available at your house. Also find out what size supply line and what size meter you have.

3. Now you are ready to pick the components for your systems. Figuring out how much area a head will cover with your water pressure and where to place each head are the difficult steps in installation. You really need qualified dealer assistance to design an efficient system.

Your local lawn-sprinkler dealer can also advise you on whether you should have a hydraulic system (automatic valves activated by water pressure) or an electric system (automatic valves activated by electricity).

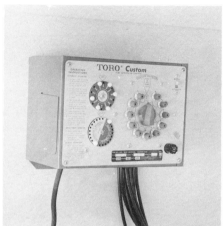 

Left: The controller is plugged into an electric outlet with the cord at the left. The other tubing runs to the automatic valves. *Right:* Your hardware or sprinkler dealer will make up the valve system needed for your property. All you do is attach it to the outside faucet.

4. Mount the controller, the brain of the system, on a wall indoors or in a sheltered spot outside. The garage is generally the best location since a neighbor can then turn off the system if you are away during prolonged periods of rain.

5. Attach an automatic valve system to the outside supply line. Each valve regulates several sprinklers. Run the control lines from the controller to the automatic valves. You may have to bore a small hole through an outside wall.

If you lay the pipe on the ground and attach the heads to stakes in an upright position, you can test the system before you dig any holes.

6. Next lay the pipe for each valve section. Drive stakes into the ground to locate the sprinkler heads. Once you have put in the stakes for one section, lay out the pipe and heads above ground. Attach the heads upright onto the stakes and connect the pipe. This way you can test the section before you do any digging. Also testing will soften the soil for easier digging. If you have made a mistake, you can catch it before you begin cutting up your lawn.

Power equipment will make the job of laying pipe easier, but if you are doing the job by hand, a straight-edged shovel will help. Cut a wedge-shaped slit in the ground about 6 inches deep for the pipe.

Power equipment for laying pipe, like this trencher, can be rented from local dealers.

The plastic pipe of underground sprinkler systems can be cut with a knife but lasts longer than old-fashioned galvanized or copper pipe. Sprinkler heads can be attached to the pipe with a simple screwdriver.

7. At the location of each sprinkler head, dig a hole 10 to 12 inches deep for a drain valve. Fill this partially with gravel or small stones for drainage. Connection of the sprinkler head to the pipe is relatively easy. Since you are using plastic pipe, it can be cut with a sharp knife. All manufacturers supply instructional material and most include simple coupling devices that require only a screwdriver for tightening clamps.

8. Once the pipe is installed and buried, adjust the heads to cover the exact area desired and to set the controller.

9. Test the system by placing a tin can on the lawn. Measure the amount of water deposited in the can in one hour and use this as a basis for your schedule. Your dealer can tell you how many inches of water a week are needed to keep your grass green.

10. Finally set the automatic controls. These operate like a clock. Pegs on the dial indicate the time the watering cycle or cycles should begin. The length of the cycle for each sprinkler head can also be specifically controlled, usually from 0 to 60 minutes for each cycle. Thus, sprinklers covering areas requiring more or less water can be programmed accordingly. Once the schedule is set, you can sit back and forget watering problems.

Once the system has been installed, tested and scheduled, it will keep your lawn healthy and green whether you are at home or on a South Seas vacation.

CHAPTER XI

‹reretererererererer›

WHERE NOT

TO HAVE A LAWN

‹reretererererererer› If grass won't grow in an area because of too much shade, if a slope is too steep or too rocky to mow, if you have too much lawn and already enough permanent surfacing, this chapter has your answers: mulches and special plants to use as low-upkeep ground coverings.

Where a mulch—such as wood chips, stones, or pebbles—can be used, the least possible upkeep results. Spread it over bare spaces between trees, shrubs, or in flower beds. A good mulch conserves soil moisture, stabilizes soil temperatures, and keeps down weeds.

Select a mulch material on the basis of availability and appearance. Subdued earth colors are best. The light color of, say, white gravel can become a glaring distraction. The idea is that a mulch will save time, produce better plants, and be of pleasant appearance. Fresh sawdust takes so much nitrogen from the soil that you have to add about a pound of nitrogen to each 100 pounds of dry sawdust you put down. But if sawdust is plentiful in your area, and inexpensive, it may be worth your while to use it and add the fertilizer. Never put down a mulch that is likely to contain weed seeds—straw, for example, which might have bindweed or other noxious weeds. Know your source.

In recent years the mulching trend has been to small stones, gravel, or wood chips. Hardwood bark chips make an ideal organic mulch, easy to apply and maintain. They are not costly, and with a little aging turn a rich dark brown. Chips vary from $1.50 to $3.50 for 3 cubic feet, enough to cover 9 square feet 4 inches deep. Apply at any time. These chips also make natural-looking paths and walkways and are useful under children's play equipment.

To make the most effective use of a mulch, first clear the area to be covered. Remove all weeds. Then lay black or clear plastic over the area. Make cutouts around existing plants or, after laying

**To make a large property manageable, Robert Zion
used English ivy in great free-form beds, with gravel
paths. The foreground shows edge of outdoor living
area, paved with bricks in jack-in-jack pattern.** *Howland Associates photo.*

the plastic, make holes where plants are to be inserted in the soil.
Then spread the mulch. Plastic keeps weeds to an absolute minimum, yet adequate moisture seeps in around plants and through
the places where strips overlap. If the terrain is steeply sloped,
wood chips will not stay in place; then planting with a bank-
binding plant is your answer (see later in this chapter).

Heavy tar roofing paper is also used to keep out weeds in an
area of trees and shrubs. Camouflage this unattractive material
with wood chips, stones, pebbles, or gravel. Edge the area with a
brick mowing strip, preferably set with mortar, so that hand-trim-
ming will not be needed and the mulch stays cleanly where it belongs, not mixing in with the grass, or spilling into the walkway.

Another helpful place for a mulch is along the drip-strip of a house that does not have guttering. Gravel, or another absorbent mulch, such as redwood bark chips, laid 6 to 10 inches deep, soaks up the runoff immediately, and permits the use of the strip area as a walkway—instead of making it a place where plants are beaten to the ground in an ugly strip of eroded soil.

Some warnings about mulch materials: *Dry* peatmoss can be impermeable to water. Dry peat and straw can be fire hazards. Lawn-grass clippings belong nowhere except on the compost heap. To take them directly from the mower and place on a flower bed is to invite disease and a most unpleasant odor. In windy climates, cocoa-bean and buckwheat hulls may blow away.

GROUND-COVERS

Ground-covers are fine where grass is difficult to grow or mow, as on a steep slope or in heavy shade.

The best plants for the purpose make a solid cover. They should be of a type to propagate easily, generally growing not above 12 inches, and in most situations, sturdy enough to be walked over at least occasionally. The best ground-cover plants thrive in a wide range of soil and moisture conditions, and are relatively free of pests and disease. Three kinds that meet these requirements are myrtle (*Vinca minor*), pachysandra, and English ivy. These and others are discussed at the end of this chapter.

After selecting a ground-cover, prepare the soil as well as your strength, time, and money allow. Good preparation eventually means less work. Work in fertilizer; 3 to 6 pounds of a 5-10-5 to each 100 square feet will do nicely. Incorporate plenty of peatmoss, well-rotted manure, leafmold, sand, or compost, particularly in sticky soil. Add lots of extra humus if the soil is sandy. If you can't manage this preparation over the entire area, then improve the soil for each planting hole.

Determine how close to plant. If quick cover and erosion prevention are your aim, set plants close together, for example, 12 inches for English ivy and pachysandra. For very steep or difficult areas, choose a creeper that roots at the nodes, English ivy, for example, or a woody plant with an abundance of horizontal, ground-hugging stems; Hall's honeysuckle is good but can become a pest if growing conditions are too encouraging.

Ground-covers can be a natural extension of a clipped lawn area, but for a neat appearance with less upkeep, design clean divisions between the casual ground-cover habit and the clipped formality of a lawn. Consider pachysandra. Never was there a more widely planted ground-cover, except English ivy. Yet pachysandra gets a bad name when it is allowed to spread into a straggly line at the lawn's edge. It needs a structural outline, a brick or metal mowing strip, so that it can't wander carelessly into the grass.

Creeping junipers give this entry area year-round color without upkeep. A mulch of marble chips conserves soil moisture and keeps down weeds.

Wherever you have a large expanse of ground-cover, it is possible to interplant with spring-flowering bulbs. For deep ground-cover—to 10 inches tall—select the taller daffodils. In a flat, low ground-cover, plant grape-hyacinths, crocus, scilla, and chionodoxa. You may also interplant fall-blooming crocus, colchicum, and sternbergia.

The cost of a ground-cover for a large area can be prohibitive, but you can always start with a few plants, and propagate them by cuttings or division. For these starter plants, prepare the soil extra well, keep it moist, and feed lightly but frequently to get rapid growth. Of course, if your neighbor has an established stand of a choice ground-cover that needs thinning, you can do him a favor by carefully pulling out some of the older plants for your own use.

PERENNIAL GROUND-COVERS

Aegopodium podagraria variegatum. GOUTWEED. Deciduous. Sun or shade. Spreads by creeping rootstock; 12–15 inches high. A nearly indestructible plant, or, in other words, a terrible weed except for unlimited areas.

Ajuga reptans. BUGLE-WEED. Evergreen to semi-evergreen. Sun or shade. Spreads by stolons; 4–8 inches high. When established, discourages weeds. Forms dense mat. For quick cover, space 6 inches apart. Flowers in attractive purple, blue, or white spikes in spring.

Asarum canadense. WILD GINGER. Evergreen. Shade. Spreads by underground rootstock; 6–8 inches high. Attractive kidney-shaped, cupped leaves. Thrives in moist, rich, woodsy soil.

Asperula odorata. SWEET WOODRUFF. Deciduous. Partial to full shade. Succulent, fresh green leaves give off pleasant scent of new-mown hay when crushed underfoot; 8 inches high. Excellent in rocky, wooded areas.

Bergenia cordifolia. Deciduous. Sun to partial shade. Creeping clumps form colonies of thick, heavy leaves; 12 inches high. Excellent in moist, woodsy, wild situation.

Callirhoe involucrata. BUFFALO-ROSE or POPPY-MALLOW. Deciduous. Sun. Trailing plants; 6–8 inches high. Lobed leaves like a

To give the owner time to enjoy this tranquil garden, the lawn has been replaced with no-upkeep pachysandra, a refreshing green ground-cover. *George Taloumis photo.*

true geranium. Dark-crimson flowers 2 inches across in summer. Plant divisions in spring. Extremely deep-rooted; drought tolerant.

Ceratostigma plumbaginoides. PLUMBAGO or LEADWORT. Deciduous to semi-evergreen. Sun to partial shade. Creeping stems; 6 inches high. Abundant blue flowers in early fall. Foliage does not appear until late spring.

Comptonia peregrina. SWEET-FERN. Deciduous shrub; 3 feet. Sun. Bank-binder. Transplant from the wild with lots of roots. Keep moist until established. Aromatic foliage.

Convallaria majalis. LILY-OF-THE-VALLEY. Deciduous. Open or deep shade, but not much bloom without some sun. Well-established plants spread rapidly by underground rootstocks; leaves 6–8 inches high. White, fragrant flowers in spring. Should not be walked on.

Cornus canadensis. BUNCHBERRY. Evergreen. Shade in moist, peaty soil. Starry white flowers in late spring. Creeps by underground rootstock; 6–8 inches high. Thrives in cold climates.

Coronilla varia. CROWN VETCH. Deciduous. Sun. Sprawling, billowy clumps; 24 inches high. Pink and white flowers. Excellent in any soil; fine choice for rough areas; bank-binder; erosion controller. Can readily be grown from seed or division.

Dianthus deltoides. MAIDEN PINK. Deciduous to semi-evergreen. Sun. Creeping, mat-forming; 6-8 inches high. Flowers in early summer, and sometimes later through season. Can also be increased by seed.

Epimedium macranthum. BARRENWORT. Deciduous (foliage browns in fall but persists through winter). Shade. Spreads; 9-12 inches high. Elegant and airy, best in moist, woodsy soil.

Euphorbia cyparissias. CYPRESS SPURGE. Deciduous. Sun. Spreads quickly; 8-10 inches high. Rough, dry areas; steep banks. Tends to woodiness, but useful in the right place.

Fragaria chiloensis (or hybrids). STRAWBERRY. Deciduous to semi-evergreen. Sun. Spreads by stolons and forms a dense mat 3-6 inches high. Needs thinning every two or three years.

Lysimachia nummularia. MONEYWORT, CREEPING CHARLEY, CREEPING JENNY. Deciduous. Sun or shade. Creeper, 2-3 inches high. Yellow flowers in summer. Tends to spread and mix into the lawn unless curbed.

Hemerocallis. DAYLILY. Perennial, mostly deciduous; some less cold-hardy varieties are evergreen in the South. Sun to partial shade. Grassy clumps, to 24 inches high, with flowering stems rising taller in season. Excellent bank-binder; may be used to control area where erosion is a problem, if planted 12-18 inches apart, and established at first by rocks or logs placed at intervals.

Liriope muscari. LILY-TURF. Evergreen. Winter-hardy south of Washington. Sun or shade. Spreads by underground stems. Coarse, grassy clumps, 10-15 inches high. Lavender flowers in August.

Mitchella repens. PARTRIDGE-BERRY. Evergreen. Shade, even dense. Creeping stems take root along the ground; 4-6 inches high. White

A maintenance-free ground-cover of evergreen pachysandra replaces the front lawn on this property. A border of hardy perennial hostas grows next to the house wall. When the grade was changed during construction, a brick well was built to save the old shade tree. Robert Zion, L. A. *Howland Associates photo.*

flowers, followed by bright red berries in early autumn. Propagate by seed or division. Grows slowly, but a beautiful ground-cover in a woody area.

Ophiopogon japonicus. DWARF LILY-TURF. Evergreen. Sun or shade. Spreads by underground stems. Grassy leaves form a sod-like mat. 8-12 inches high. Also called *Mondo japonicus.*

Pachysandra terminalis. JAPANESE SPURGE. Evergreen. Sun or shade. Spreads; 6-8 inches high. Glossy, dark green leaves. Plant 8 inches apart for quick cover. Propagate by cuttings. *P. terminalis* 'Silveredge' with white-marked leaves is interesting for a lighter shade of green to relieve a large expanse of ground-cover in a shaded area. Plants in full sun need more watering and feeding than those in shade.

Phlox subulata. MOSS-PINK. Evergreen. Sun. Creeps, each plant forming a large dense mat; 6 inches high. Flowers white or in vivid shades of pink, red, or lavender in spring. Avoid the violent magenta variety. Ideal for rocky banks where stems can cascade.

Polygonum reynowtria. FLEECE-FLOWER. Deciduous. Sun. Spreads rapidly by underground stems; 12 inches high. Sprays of lacy flowers in autumn, at first dark red, change to pink. Light green leaves turn red in autumn.

Polystichum acrostichoides. CHRISTMAS FERN or EVERGREEN FERN. Shade. Fronds to 24 inches high, form mats. Evergreen to January. Fine for rocky banks and crevices.

Ranunculus repens. CREEPING BUTTERCUP. Deciduous. Sun to partial shade. Spreads by runners; 6-8 inches high, with yellow flowers in spring on stems to 24 inches. Useful for moist places. Given a chance, it will spread into lawn areas.

Sedum. STONECROP. Evergreen (semi-evergreen in cold climates). Spreads rapidly by trailing stems, too invasive to be grown near less dominant plants. To 6 inches high. Unusually fine for dry, sun-baked places, especially *Sedum acre, S. sarmentosum,* and *S. sexangulare.*

Sempervivum. HOUSELEEK or HEN AND CHICKS. Evergreen to semi-evergreen. Sun. Spreads by offsets. Leaves form neat low rosettes. Especially useful for a sandy or rocky bank.

Thymus serpyllum. CREEPING THYME. Deciduous. Creeping stems covered by tiny leaves form large dense mats; 2-4 inches high. When stepped on, gives off a pleasing fragrance. *T. s. coccineum,* with reddish purple flowers in late June, is probably the best of all thymes for covering ground in sunny, hot, dry places. Evergreen leaves turn bronze in autumn.

Veronica latifolia. CREEPING VERONICA. Deciduous. Sun to partial shade. Spreads by creeping stems; 4-6 inches high. Pale-blue flowers in June over dark foliage. *V. rupestris* spreads into a solid mat; gives sapphire-blue flowers in May and June. Drought tolerant; competes well with weeds.

Vinca minor. PERIWINKLE or MYRTLE. Evergreen. Partial to full shade. (In sun, winter burn may be a problem.) Needs fertile, humusy, moist soil for best results.

Viola (*V. odorata* and various American species). HARDY VIOLET. Deciduous. Will grow in full shade, but won't bloom as much as in partial sun. Native violets make excellent ground-covers in shaded moist places. Self-sow abundantly; given opportunity, they do spread into lawn areas, otherwise they are easy to grow, and pleasant throughout the growing season. Need ample water in late summer.

WOODY GROUND-COVERS (subshrubs)

Arctostaphylos uva-ursi. BEARBERRY. Evergreen. Sun to partial shade. Creeper; 4-8 inches high. Dark green leaves. Grows well by the ocean in sandy soils. Sometimes difficult to get started.

Calluna vulgaris. HEATHER. Evergreen. Sun. Upright, shrub to 12 inches high. Needle-like leaves. Prune out old wood in the spring. Soil on the acid side, humusy. Spikes of pink flowers in autumn.

Cotoneaster dammeri radicans. LITTLELEAF COTONEASTER. Evergreen. Sun. Prostrate creeper; 12 inches high. Excellent on banks or other large areas. Also *C. horizontalis* (PROSTRATE or ROCK COTONEASTER). Semi-evergreen to deciduous.

Erica carnea. HEATH. Evergreen. Sun. Spreading or upright shrubs; to 12 inches high. Very small leaves. Spikes of white or rose-pink flowers in early spring. Needs soil on the acid side, humusy and well drained. Clip out dead wood in the spring after flowering.

Euonymus fortunei. WINTERCREEPER. Evergreen. Sun to partial shade. Trailer, 10 inches high. Heavy, dark green foliage. Variety *coloratus* has vivid reddish purple leaves in autumn. *Minimus* has tiny leaves. *Reticulatus* has variegated green-and-white leaves. Use on slopes and banks. Will eventually climb walls and trees, by means of aerial rootlets.

Gaultheria procumbens. WINTERGREEN. Evergreen. Light shade. Creeper; 3 inches high. Small, shiny leaves. Thrives in rich, moist soil in woods.

Hedera helix. ENGLISH IVY. Evergreen. Sun to shade. *Hedera helix baltica* (BALTIC IVY) is hardiest, and recommended for colder climates. Plant well-rooted cuttings 12 inches apart. If stems are long enough, pin them down with wire bent to hairpin form, or hold down with small stones, so that roots along the stems will take hold. The old saying about ivy is worth remembering: The first year it sleeps, the second it creeps, and the third it grows by leaps. It burns if exposed to winter sun but recovers if cut back in spring. Moist, humusy soil is conducive to luxuriant growth.
Helianthemum nummularium. SUN-ROSE. Sun. 6-12 inches high. Use in a dry place.

Hypericum calycinum. ST. JOHN'S-WORT. Sun to partial shade. Clumps spread by underground rootstocks; 18 inches high; for bank-binding. Yellow flowers in summer.

Iberis sempervirens. HARDY CANDYTUFT. Evergreen, Sun to partial shade. Clumps of dark green leaves, 6-8 inches high, spread apart with age to reveal woody stems. White flowers in spring. Tolerates drought.

Leiophyllum buxifolium. SAND-MYRTLE. Evergreen. Sun to light shade. Low, spreading shrub; 12 inches high. Can be grown from seed. Needs acid, humusy soil enriched with sand and peatmoss.

Pachistima canbyi. PACHISTIMA. Evergreen. Sun or shade. Woody spreading plant; 8-12 inches high. Small, dark green leaves. Prefers rich soil on the acid side. Sometimes slow to get established.

Teucrium chamaedrys. GERMANDER. Evergreen. Sun to partial shade. Upright little bushes, 8-12 inches high. Dark green leaves.

LARGE VINES AND RAMBLERS

Akebia quinata. FIVELEAF AKEBIA. Deciduous. Sun. Woody vine to use as a ground-cover; 12 inches high. Keep it away from trees and shrubs as it will gain hold on and twine around. Curious flowers not showy; but elegant foliage.

Lonicera japonica. JAPANESE HONEYSUCKLE. Semi-evergreen. Sun to partial shade. Fragrant flowers, white changing to yellow. For large banks and steep slopes. Stem-roots help bind soil, prevent erosion. When growth gets rampant, chop back ruthlessly in spring. *L. henryi* is less invasive, and tends to be evergreen.

Rosa. ROSE. Climbers or ramblers of the *R. wichuraiana* type make excellent and tough ground-covers. Deciduous. Sun. Trail on the ground, to 24 inches high. Some kinds form roots along the stems where they touch moist soil. Excellent bank-binder in large, sloping area.

DWARF NEEDLE-LEAVED EVERGREENS

Juniperus (low-growing forms). PROSTRATE JUNIPER. Sun. Spreading growth, 8–20 inches high. *J. horizontalis* has blue-green foliage; its cultivar *procumbens* is the CREEPING JUNIPER, only a few inches high. Also excellent: *J. squamata, J. conferta,* and *J. chinensis sargenti,* all with light-green or gray-green foliage.

Taxus (low-growing forms). YEW. Sun to partial shade. Spreading, about 12 inches high. Use *T. baccata repandens* (SPREADING ENGLISH YEW), or *T. canadensis stricta* (DWARF SPREADING CANADA YEW). All yews have very dark green leaves.

CHAPTER XII

ᒫᒬᒫᒬᒫᒬᒫᒬᒫᒬᒫᒬᒬ

TOOLS

TO KEEP THE UPKEEP DOWN

ᒫᒬᒫᒬᒫᒬᒫᒬᒫᒬᒫᒬᒫᒬᒫᒬ   The ultimate tool for low upkeep is still a good yard man. Unfortunately, a good yard man is hard to find—and very expensive. But if you want Saturday afternoons free, don't resort to green concrete. Instead, tool-up properly to help keep maintenance down.

MOWING EQUIPMENT

The power mower industry offers the prospective buyer a wide, and sometimes confusing, variety of equipment. Reels and rotaries, riders and tractors, self-propelled and hand-propelled. Which type is best for your lawn? The mower you choose will be your working partner for many a summer, so it pays to match it carefully to the size and shape of your lawn.

ROTARY. The king-pin of powered mowers is definitely the rotary. About ten rotary mowers are sold for every reel mower. Rotary mowers enjoy tremendous popularity because of relatively low price and easy maintenance. They do an excellent job of cutting tall grass and weeds, and are effective for cutting both fine and coarse grasses.

Because of their broad base and usual floating suspension, rotaries can be used on rough ground and tend to hide low spots by maintaining an even cutting level. The best-designed models have blades that extend beyond the wheels. This does away with hand trimming along flower beds and around shrubbery.

Some rotaries have a special housing that produces a vacuuming action. They can clean lawns of spring debris, permitting grass to "green" earlier. They cut and bag grass clippings and they mulch or bag autumn leaves.

134

Relatively low price and easy maintenance have made the rotary mower the most popular grass cutter. It can be used to cut and catch grass clippings in spring and summer, and to mulch and bag leaves in autumn. No tugging at a rope is needed to start the model shown. Just turn the key and it starts purring.

As more and more women take over the chores of lawn maintenance, a simple sure-start becomes a necessity. As a result, electric key starting is increasing in popularity.

In recent years, fully electric power mowers have gained in acceptance. They are favorites with the ladies since they don't have to be filled with gas and are the easiest models to operate. They simply plug in and go. They are especially good if your lawn area is fairly small and you want a mower that makes very little noise. (There is, however, a slight tendency to mow the cord along with the lawn!)

If you have a small lawn that you want to fuss with, the reel mower cuts cleanly for that manicured look. Self-propelled models are more expensive, but they give you more time for the golf course and less back trouble.

REEL MOWERS. If you have a small stand of grass and want that tailored, putting-green look, consider the powered reel mowers.

The reel mower can be set to cut down to ½ inch or less. Most quality reels have five or six blades. They cut on the scissors principle, and shear evenly and cleanly. Testing has shown that a reel mower is best for steep slopes or terraced lawns, but not effective on rough terrain.

The reel is considered safer than the rotary because it does not have a flat blade turning at high velocity. However, the blade is difficult to sharpen and, when damaged, hard to repair.

Reel and rotary mowers come in both hand- and self-propelled models. Self-propelled models are, of course, higher priced, but they do reduce mowing time and make the whole job easier.

RIDING MOWERS.   More and more Americans are sitting down
on the job when it comes to grass cutting. Riding mowers and
suburban tractors add fun to the whole operation. Perched astride
his tractor, a simple suburban homeowner is transformed into a
country squire, master of all he surveys. In addition to the sense
of power, akin to owning a sports car, a rider becomes a time-
saving, efficient, and labor-saving agent for mowing large areas.
Unless your lot is at least a quarter acre in size, however, leave
the driving to someone else.

A riding mower is strictly a grass cutter. The cutting unit is
permanently attached. A rider with a 36-inch rotary cutting unit
can mow a 100- × 100-foot lawn in forty minutes. The horsepower
of the rider is less than that of a tractor, and so is the price. For
versatility, as a yard workhorse, look at the garden tractors.

**Add a little fun to grass cutting with a riding mower
or tractor. They save both time and effort. However,
if you don't have at least a quarter acre of grass,
leave the driving to someone with a larger property.**

Tractors for home use are commonly divided into lawn and suburban types. Seven horsepower or below is the lawn class. Ten or above rates as a suburban tractor.

Tractors take care of a large mowing area and can also clear away snow, plough, till, fertilize, and cart. Homeowners with wooded acreage can use them to haul out felled trees or to take rubbish to the dump. The more attachments you acquire for lawn-care chores, the more help you will realize from your investment. A tractor saves both time and labor, so keep it busy.

No matter what type mower you pick, the best guide to satisfaction is to buy from a reputable servicing dealer. Get the best mower you can afford and the biggest size practical. The larger the mower, the faster the mowing.

HAND TOOLS

When nagged to perform household chores, the refrain of husbands around the world has always been either, "I haven't the time," or "I haven't the right tools."

With the increase in leisure, time is becoming an improbable excuse. Tools, well—that's a different story.

Lack of tools may still be a ploy, but even the most exasperated wife won't deny that proper tools are vital for any home project. The right tools can cut work in half. This is especially true when it comes to lawn and garden care.

LAWN TOOLS

BROOM RAKE. A broad, curved rake of bamboo or metal. You need one; but there are easier, faster ways to sweep leaves and lawn debris.

STEEL RAKE. Used for smoothing newly turned soil, and for clearing lawns of debris heavier than leaves or grass clippings—gravel, chunks of sod, earth-laden weeds, and so on.

LAWN SWEEPER. Available in hand-operated models, or as attachments for powered mowing equipment. Far easier than broom rakes for picking up grass clippings and clearing the lawn of leaves.

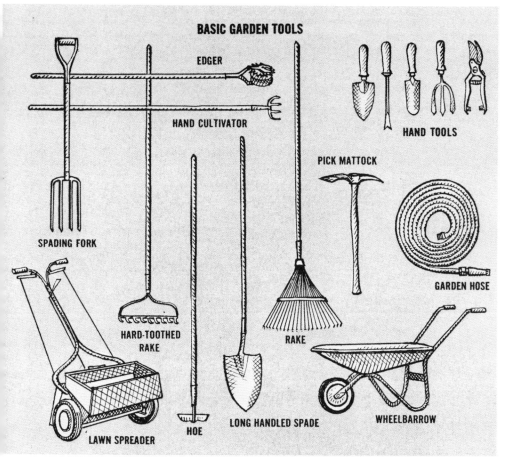

From *The Bissell Home Handbook of Gardening*, by permission.

SPREADER. The hopper spreader, powered by you, is the most popular tool for distribution of fertilizers, lime, grass seed, and granular chemicals for lawns. It is essential for even application.

"V"-CUT WEEDER. This is a hand tool, either long- or short-handled, designed to simplify the cutting out of tap-rooted weeds such as dandelion.

WATERING DEVICES.   If you don't have an underground sprinkling system, you will need an overground sprinkling system—
in other words, several lengths of hose and some watering devices.
Plastic hoses are generally less expensive than rubber and are also
lighter to handle. But, they are more susceptible, if left filled with
water, to freezing. They also kink more easily, shutting off the water supply. All hoses have standard couplings that fit any sprinkler.

Many types of sprinklers are on the market; some depend on
water pressure to achieve maximum efficiency. Discuss this aspect
and your watering needs with the local hardware dealer, or garden
supply man, before you buy.

For watering trees and shrubbery, soakers are recommended,
either the long, hoselike fabric soakers that dribble water into the
ground, or perforated plastic soakers.

LAWN EDGERS.   Mowing strips keep edging at a minimum. If
you edge only once or twice a season, a hand model is fine. If
you must have a "fine edged" lawn, consider a powered edger.

TRIMMERS.   Hand-operated grass shears or clippers do a good
job on grass to be trimmed from the base of lamp posts, mail
boxes, fences, steps, and walls. But here again power equipment
will save time and take the ache out of the job. Keep the need to
use a trimmer at a minimum with mowing strips and edging materials.

TOOLS FOR HEDGE AND SHRUBBERY MAINTENANCE

PRUNING SHEARS.   You will use these often, for everything
from the shaping of dwarf fruit trees to the cutting down of old
sunflowers, so buy the best pair available. Many gardeners prefer
the anvil type.

BUSH-HOOKS.   These do jobs too big for the pruning shears,
and are handy when it comes to trimming prickly rose hedges and
barberry. Smaller properties can usually do without, so wait until
you have a real and frequent need before you invest.

LOPPING SHEARS.   This tool will allow you to clip away
branches too high to reach with a bush-hook or a saw, and is a
must if you live in a wooded area.

HEDGE SHEARS. Electric shears make the symmetrical pruning of shrubs and hedges simple and are a good investment even when the amount of hedge to be trimmed is minimal.

SPRAY UNIT. There are many types available to distribute pesticides and liquid fertilizers. A small, simple, hand-operated gun is all you need to care for low-growing shrubs and plantings, but to spray mature trees, you will have to have a tank and spray gun. The alternative is to hire a professional to do it for you on a yearly basis, and if yours is a property of any size, this is worth doing.

TREE FEEDER. This is useful only if you have a number of trees in need of special attention. Among the more popular feeders are the hollow-tube types that bring dry or liquid fertilizers down to tree-root levels.

WATERING DEVICES. See under Lawn Tools above.

PLANTING TOOLS

SHOVEL, SPADE. A shovel is curved to contain loose earth or gravel, while a spade is flat, slides more readily into the soil, and is used to lift clods, compacted earth, root balls, and for digging and turning garden soil. Both are necessities for the gardener.

SPADING FORK. A variation on the spade, a spading fork can be pushed more easily than a spade into hard, compacted, or heavily rooted earth.

RAKE. See Lawn Tools.

HAND TROWEL. This is the tool for transplanting seedlings, setting out bulbs, and digging small planting holes. Invest in a heavy-duty one, not a 69-cent one stamped out of cheap metal. A good trowel lasts for a generation.

PICK MATTOCK. When the ground is hard or rocky, this tool can be a planter's best friend.

CULTIVATOR. A small claw-shaped cultivator makes digging up weeds around plants easy. For garden-size jobs, a long-handled cultivator is necessary. However, with the use of mulch to keep weeds out, you shouldn't need the larger model.

Hoe. A pointed, long-handled hoe is useful for cutting out weeds and for marking planting rows in flower and vegetable gardens. A square-ended hoe serves similar purposes.

Pail. Every garden needs a plastic or galvanized metal pail for use in transplanting and to water young trees and shrubs when the hose isn't handy.

String and Pegs. A long, sturdy string tied to two long, sharply-pointed pegs makes a row marker to help you keep planting rows straight.

Wheelbarrow. A necessity. Check for good balance and sturdy construction.

Board. One of the simpler accessories is a wooden board. Use this to walk on when working with newly turned loam or on new lawns, otherwise you will compact the soil.

Ties. Raffia- or plastic-covered metal ties, either in precut lengths or in a continuous roll, make staking of shrubs, flowers, and vegetables easy.

Markers. It is amazingly easy to forget what you planted where, and when. Plastic or wooden markers labeled with indelible ink save a lot of confusion.

CARE OF TOOLS

Homeowners who take proper care of garden tools are a small minority. Most dispose of them far sooner than necessary, simply because they don't take a few minutes at the end of fall to clean and oil their equipment.

Mothball your garden tools by first removing all rust and dirt with a wire brush or an emery cloth. Sharpen all blades, hoes, and shovels. Coat metal parts with asphalt varnish or heavy grease to prevent rust, particularly if they are to be stored where there is humidity, as in an unheated garage or tool shed.

Tighten any loose handles. It wouldn't hurt to coat wooden handles with linseed oil.

Your power equipment will carry instructions for maintenance and storage. Follow it—you're protecting your investment.

NATURAL TOOLS

Why not let Mother Nature help with your garden and land-scaping chores? After all, she's an expert when it comes to growing things.

Ants, grubs, beetles, worms, and wild bees aerate the soil as they burrow. Earth-dwelling insects enrich the ground just by their presence and many help it by burying decaying vegetable matter.

Actually the best natural help to low-maintenance landscaping comes from insects. Not all insects, mind you, but a friendly few can be helpful in destroying plant pests. In the forefront of man's best gardening friends are dragonflies, damselflies, aphid lions, ground beetles, ladybugs, syrphid flies, and praying mantises. Learn to recognize and protect these creatures.

Whether you call them darning needles or dragonflies, they devour a lot of mosquitoes and other small insects. There are over 300 species in the United States. Gauzy-winged and brilliantly colored, they live around ponds, lakes, and swamps.

The damselfly is smaller and more delicate than the dragonfly, and has a more leisurely flight. When at rest, its wings are folded back. The young thrive on mosquito larvae.

The daily diet of an aphid lion consists of 200 to 400 aphids. When the odd grayish brown lion turns into the delicate lacewing with beautiful golden eyes and long antennae, its diet includes the eggs of caterpillars, all stages of plant-feeding mites, scale insects, and mealy bugs as well as aphids.

Ground beetles feed almost entirely on other insects, including ants and termites, and on snails. They're happiest when under a stone. Can't fly, but they sure can scurry.

Her gluttonous appetite may not be ladylike, but the ladybug is a helpful ally. Adults and larvae eat tremendous numbers of aphids, scales, and other soft-bodied plant-damaging insects.

Sluglike larvae of syrphid flies are effective killers of various plant pests, especially aphids. The adult usually has a banded body and sounds like a bee when in the air.

An odd-looking relative of the grasshopper, the praying mantis feeds irreligiously on insects in both its nymphal and adult stages. A voracious eater.

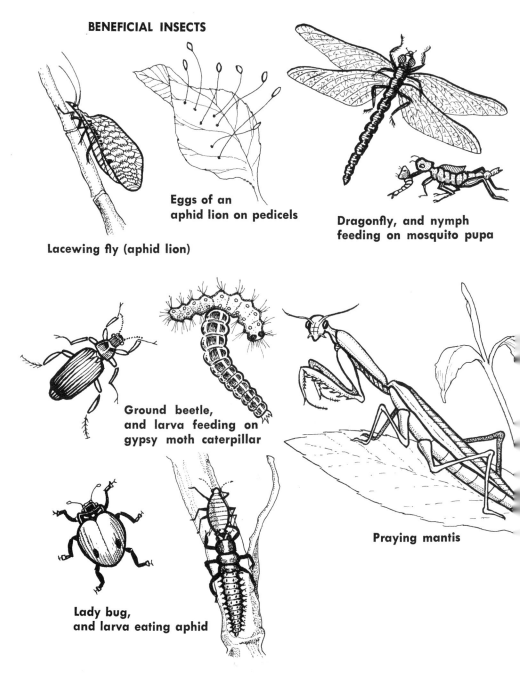

BENEFICIAL INSECTS

Eggs of an aphid lion on pedicels

Lacewing fly (aphid lion)

Dragonfly, and nymph feeding on mosquito pupa

Ground beetle, and larva feeding on gypsy moth caterpillar

Praying mantis

Lady bug, and larva eating aphid

144

INDEX

145